THE
PRESIDENT'S
MEDAL
1789-
1977

The portrait model of President Jimmy Carter's inaugural medal for 1977,
in the original plaster, by the Georgia sculptor Julian Hoke Harris
© 1977 the Inaugural Committee
The Franklin Mint

THE PRESIDENT'S MEDAL
1789·1977

BY NEIL MACNEIL

Clarkson N. Potter, Inc./Publisher NEW YORK
In association with the National Portrait Gallery, Smithsonian Institution

DISTRIBUTED BY CROWN PUBLISHERS, INC.

Designed by Stephen Kraft

Library of Congress Cataloging in Publication Data

MacNeil, Neil, 1927–
The President's medal, 1789–1977.

Includes index.
1. Presidents—United States—Medals—Exhibitions.
2. Presidents—United States—Inauguration—Exhibitions.
I. National Portrait Gallery, Washington, D. C.
II. Title.
CJ5802.2.W37M3   1977   745   76-49563
ISBN 0-517-52917-3
ISBN 0-517-52918-1 pbk.

An effort was made to reproduce all medals at their actual size, with
the exception of those less than 38 millimeters in diameter. These
were enlarged for the sake of legibility.

CONTENTS

ACKNOWLEDGMENTS

The quest that produced this study began as a lark. I have long been fascinated by what Joseph Conrad called the plasticity of sculpture, especially the effects that a master can work in bronze. This led to my interest in the bas-reliefs of the greatest of American sculptors, Augustus Saint-Gaudens, and that, in turn, brought me to an awareness of the medals struck to commemorate the inaugurations of the Presidents of the United States. Saint-Gaudens designed one such medal for President Theodore Roosevelt in 1905. I discovered that over the life of the American Republic, Saint-Gaudens and other sculptors had given us something more than a collection of contemporary portraits of the men who have assumed the presidency: they had created an American art form worth the noting. These medals mark the ritual, repeated every four years, through which this nation refreshes its commitment to free government.

I have received help from many, not least of whom were the sculptors who designed these medals: Carl Paul Jennewein, Walker Hancock, Philip Kraczkowski, Felix de Weldon, Gilroy Roberts, Mico Kaufman, and Frank Eliscu. I owe thanks to Joseph C. McGarraghy, Edward H. Foley, Dale Miller, and J. Willard Marriott, all of whom chaired presidential inaugural committees, and to Gilbert Hahn, Jr., Bruce Sundlun, Melvin Payne, and Mark O. Hatfield, all of whom chaired inaugural medals committees.

I have special debts to Leonard W. Hall, Alfons Landa, D. B. Hardeman, James A. Councilor, John Manship, Marjorie Menconi, Pauline Manship Natti, Mrs. Lowell Ditzen, Herbert Collins, James F. Dicke II, Samuel T. Clements, Kenneth Broyles, Donald A. Schwartz, William Louth, James Harper, Albert Bush-Brown, Bradford Ross, J. Anthony Moran, Corinne Boggs, Robert Strauss, Richard B. Dusterberg, George Fuld, Harry X. Boosel, Marguerite Woolley, Lucy de Graffenried List, Cary Grayson, Jr., and Darrell C. Crain, Jr. Elvira Clain-Stefanelli and R. Le Gette Burris of the Numismatics Collection at the Smithsonian Institution showed me every courtesy, as did Mary Brooks, Director of the Bureau of the Mint, and her associates, Frank H. MacDonald, Eleanor Hayden, and Frank Gasparro. H. Joseph Levine, a specialist in this field, assisted me in many ways.

Dr. Julian Boyd and his colleague, Ruth Lester, provided important documentation on the Reich medal of Thomas Jefferson, as did S. P. Witham. The research of R. W. Julian on medals struck by the United States Mint proved useful. John Dryfhout, curator of the Saint-Gaudens National Historic Site at Cornish, New Hampshire, offered encouragement as well as help. I appreciate the help of Dr. Edmund Sullivan, curator of the DeWitt Collection at the University of Hartford, Dwight Miller of the Herbert Hoover presidential library at West Branch, Iowa, Daniel J. Reed, Director of the Presidential Libraries, National Archives and Records Service, and Stephen T. Riley, Director of the Massachusetts Historical Society.

I received assistance also from the staffs of the rare book room and manuscript division of the Library of Congress, the National Archives and Records Service, the District of Columbia Historical Society, the Franklin D. Roosevelt Library at Hyde Park, the University of Wyoming Library, the United States Department of State, the Baker Library at Dartmouth College, the John Carter Brown Library at Brown

University, Harvard University Library, the District of Columbia Public Library, the National Sculpture Society, and the American Numismatics Society.

The staff of the National Portrait Gallery helped greatly and in many ways, especially Douglas Evelyn, Beverly Cox, Michael Carrigan, Frances Wein, Suzanne Jenkins, Anne Anders, and Eugene Mantie.

To Marvin Sadik, Director of the National Portrait Gallery, I am most indebted, for it was he who brought to fruition this exhibition of inaugural medals and publication of this monograph to accompany it. An authority on medals, he contributed enthusiasm and expert knowledge as well as his managerial skill.

LENDERS TO THE EXHIBITION

Spiro T. Agnew
Alphaeus H. Albert
The American Numismatic Society, New York
Reverend Hector L. Bolduc
John Coolidge
Corcoran Gallery of Art
Darrell C. Crain, M.D.
Dartmouth College Library
Mrs. Lowell Russell Ditzen
Richard B. Dusterberg
The President and Mrs. Gerald R. Ford
The Honorable and Mrs. Gilbert Hahn, Jr.
Mr. & Mrs. Leonard W. Hall
University of Hartford
Herbert Hoover Presidential Library
Lyndon Baines Johnson Library
John F. Kennedy Library
Library of Congress
Massachusetts Historical Society
The Pierpont Morgan Library
Museum of Fine Arts, Boston
Division of Political History,
The National Museum of History and Technology,
Smithsonian Institution
Mrs. Nelson A. Rockefeller
Franklin D. Roosevelt Library
Bradford Ross
The Stark County Historical Society, Canton, Ohio
United States Department of the Interior,
National Park Service,
Saint-Gaudens National Historic Site
United States Mint
The George Washington University Library,
The Darrell C. Crain Collection of the
Official Inaugural Medals of the Presidents
and Vice Presidents of the United States of America
Woodrow Wilson House,
National Trust for Historic Preservation
in the United States

I dedicate this book to my daughter,
Deirdre MacNeil

INTRODUCTION

Although the modern medal belongs to a tradition which began with Italian Renaissance medals of the fifteenth century, the ultimate origins of medallic art go back to ancient times when large commemorative pieces, coin-like but not intended as money, were issued primarily as rewards, sometimes to be worn as decorations. Among the earliest of these objects are the Athenian silver medallions struck in commemoration of the victory at Marathon in 490 B.C. The practice continued during the Roman Empire, and imperial portrait medals were first struck for Octavianus Augustus (31 B.C.–14 A.D.). Another type of medallion—the *contorniate*—was a large copper piece with raised borders, which began to be made in the middle of the fourth century, probably to mark public games and exhibitions. These *contorniates* showed victorious athletes and mythological subjects, as well as the portraits of earlier emperors, and famous writers and poets such as Horace and Terence. Together with Roman imperial medallions, they are believed to have served as points of departure for the earliest of the Italian Renaissance medals made by Antonio Pisano, called Pisanello (circa 1395–1455), some of whose drawings after them are preserved in the Louvre.

While it should be mentioned that a few essays in medallic art were attempted in the late fourteenth century by Paduan, Venetian, and Flemish–Burgundian craftsmen, the credit for the establishment of the modern medallic tradition belongs to Pisanello. The practice quickly spread elsewhere in Italy, and continued to flourish in the sixteenth century in the hands of such exemplary medalists as the Lombard, Jacopo Nizolla da Trezzo (1515/19–1589), and into the seventeenth and eighteenth centuries, at which time perhaps the greatest Italian practitioner was the Florentine, Massimiliano Soldani-Benzi (1656–1740). During the same period, German and Dutch artists produced medals of comparable distinction. In the nineteenth century, medals which are worthy of the tradition founded by Pisanello were made by the Frenchman Pierre Jean David D'Angers (1778–1856), although these were for the most part uniface portrait plaquettes. Also worthy of mention in the nineteenth century are many of the medals produced by various members of the Wyon family in England.

The first American medals were the dozen struck to commemorate revolutionary war victories. Eleven of these were produced in France between 1780 and 1790 by three of the greatest die engravers of the Paris mint, Pierre Simon Benjamin Duvivier (1728–1819), Augustin Dupré (1748–1833), and Nicholas Marie Gatteaux (1751–1832). All but one of this group of medals was authorized by Congress to honor a particular military figure for his heroic exploits. Benjamin Franklin, then in France, probably ordered the eleventh on his own initiative, the so-called "Libertas Americana" medal, which marked the victories at Saratoga and Yorktown. The final piece in the series to honor the then Major Henry Lee for his attack on Paulus Hook, in 1779, was the only one to be produced in America by an American, Joseph Wright (1756–1793), and not until late 1792 or early 1793.

In artistic excellence and technical quality, the Lee medal is distinctly inferior to its companions made in France. The first medal made in America, in 1790, is disappointing in these same respects. Issued to mark Washington's first inaugural the year before, it is a crudely struck piece, stamped with a bizarre profile of the father of our country. It is generally referred to as the "Manly" medal, because it was first offered for sale by James (or Jacques) Manly, an Irish miniaturist and engraver, formerly resident in London, who had come tò the United States about 1789, and whose name appears on the reverse. The medal was struck by Samuel Brooks, known to have been working in Boston in 1790, possibly after a design by the Danish artist Christian Gullager, who emigrated to America in the mid-1780s, and who did a painting, and probably a bust, of Washington late in 1789.

The earliest medals produced for the federal government in the United States were intended for presentation to Indian chiefs. "Indian peace medals," as they are commonly known, were first made by the Spanish, French, and English for use in the New World; but as early as 1787, General Henry Knox, Secretary of War under the Articles of Confederation, had pointed out to Congress the desirability of having American examples to replace European prototypes. Later, Jefferson, as Secretary of State, described their purpose: "They confer no power, and seem to have taken their origin in the European practice, of giving medals or other marks of friendship to the negotiators of treaties and other diplomatic characters, or visitors of distinction." This was "an ancient custom from time immemorial."

During Washington's presidency, Indian peace medals were individually engraved on oval silver discs, the largest measuring approximately six by four inches, and were encircled by a silver ring with a loop at the top for suspension. No Indian peace medals were made during John Adams's term of office, but the practice was resumed under Jefferson. These medals were cut on steel dies by Robert Scot, an Englishman who settled in Philadelphia in 1781 and had become chief engraver at the Mint there by 1801. Each side of the medal was struck separately on thin silver discs, with the resulting hollow repoussé halves fastened together with a silver band around their edges and surmounted by a suspension loop. The portrait was based on that of Jefferson on a small medal (one-and-three quarters inches in diameter) which was made, to commemorate the President's inauguration, by John Reich (1768–1833), a German die engraver who had come to this country only the year before.

If, as seems entirely possible, the technical means did not exist in the United States for striking a large medal from a single piece of silver when the Jefferson Indian peace medal was issued, by the time the next example in the series, for James Madison—an extraordinarily perceptive likeness—was produced, in this instance by Reich, the problem no longer existed. Indeed, because the Indians themselves had reacted adversely to the light, hollow Jefferson medals, which they compared to the heavy, solid ones the British had given them, the Superintendent of Indian Trade at the time, John Mason, insisted that the Madison medals be struck from a single piece of silver.

Moritz Fürst (active in America 1808–1841), the Hungarian-born Vienna-trained die sinker, followed Reich as the maker of Indian peace medals (beginning with James Monroe) as well as other kinds of medals, including a brilliant series of twenty-six for the military heroes of the War of 1812. The obverse of one of Fürst's Indian peace medals, that for Martin Van Buren, also served, with an appropriate reverse, as the official inaugural medal for Van Buren.

In the sustained excellence evident in the work of Reich and Fürst, which forms another link in the great tradition established by Pisanello, one sees a worthy continuation of the high standards set for American medallic art by the trio of Frenchmen who produced our earliest medals.

During the 1840s and 1850s, genuinely distinguished American medals appeared less frequently. One of the finer examples in this period bears a powerful likeness of James K. Polk and adorns the obverses of both his Indian peace and inaugural medals. It is worth noting that the portrait in this case was not done by a medalist but rather by a noted American painter, John Gadsby Chapman (1808–1889). One wonders why, with the invention towards 1840 of mechanical devices to assist in the cutting of dies, coupled with the ability to reduce images in size through the use of the pantograph (known much earlier) other fine American painters and sculptors, particularly portraitists, were not employed in the noble art of medal-making. Mechanical improvements, however, would seem to have had quite the opposite effect on the production of medals. A great art form had become almost completely subservient to the influence of technical expertise and slick manufacture. While there were still consummate craftsmen in the field—men like Charles Cushing Wright (1796–1854), James Barton Longacre (1794–1869), and William Barber (1807–1879)—their great skill alone was not enough to measure up to the highest standards set for the medallic arts when they were the province of creative artists.

The shadow which had now begun to fall over the tradition of medal-making lengthened and deepened in the later nineteenth and twentieth centuries. Occasionally, however, there were bright shafts of light. Augustus Saint-Gaudens (1848–1907), one of the greatest sculptors in our history, who for nearly three decades had been making some of the finest portrait reliefs ever done by any artist anywhere, finally was called upon to do a presidential inaugural medal, that for Theodore Roosevelt in 1905. Only a few subsequent inaugural medals are even worthy of mention in such company: those done by Paul Manship (1885–1966) for Franklin D. Roosevelt's first inaugural and John F. Kennedy's (the latter have been greatly diminished in quality by the reduction in size of the image of the President in order to cut down on the number of times the die would have to be struck), by Jo Davidson (1883–1952) for Roosevelt's third and fourth inaugurals, and by Darrel C. Crain (1879–1969) for Warren G. Harding. Crain's portrait is an exceptionally sensitive and knowing likeness of his subject and stands as the finest ever done in any medium of Harding.

The first thing one wants in presidential inaugural medals, and indeed in portrait medals made for any purpose, is what Thomas L. McKenney, who headed the Bureau of Indian Affairs from 1824 to 1830, wanted for the Indian peace medals which were to be distributed under his purview. "I am certainly anxious," he wrote, "that these medals should be as perfect in their resemblance of the original, as the artist can make them. They are intended, not for the Indians, only, but for posterity." Inaugural medals indeed "should be as perfect in their resemblance of the original, as the artist can make them," not only because they mark our greatest national quadrennial event and today help to defray the expenses of the festivities for these occasions, but also, and even more important, because they "are intended . . . for posterity."

We live in a time in which, because of the ubiquitous photograph and the fact that our art academies have moved in directions other than representationalism, it might also be said that the bottom has fallen out of the nadir of portraiture. Yet there are a few noteworthy practitioners in the field capable of applying their genius to the medallic arts, and there might well be more if there were an intelligent patronage receptive to the achievements of such artists. Inaugural medals committees, which thus far have labored so admirably to preserve a great tradition, and which more lately have managed so effectively not only the production of medals but their distribution as well, should in the future include among their number at least two qualified museum directors or curators, one whose institution is devoted to art from early times to the present, and the other, to modern and contemporary art. Only if this kind of broadly based and largely disinterested expertise is brought to bear upon the selection of the artist to design the inaugural medal can there be any chance of assuring both its artistic excellence and its historical validity. Perhaps, too, the entire project ought to begin soon after those presidential contenders likely to be elected have been nominated. This would provide more ample time for the production of the inaugural medal, and allow as well for medals to be struck privately for the unsuccessful candidate or candidates. (A medal prepared in advance for Richard Nixon was so struck for some of his friends and associates after his defeat in the presidential election of 1960.)

In the Foreword of the catalog for an exhibition of medallic art held a decade ago, I wrote, *Few artifacts of any age have come down to us charged with the meaning of so many facets of their time as the Renaissance medal. Though relatively diminutive in size, they embody to an exceptional degree that fusion of art and thought which is one of the chief glories of the Renaissance. Indeed, in their beauty and their learning, these medals are a reflection in microcosm of the civilization which produced them . . . and they have been preserved down through the years by those who have cherished them as enduring expressions of the Humanistic tradition.* Given the greatness of this land—in spite of all its faults—and the exceptional achievements already encompassed by the arts in America in the twentieth century, it is my hope that what can be said of Renaissance medals may one day be said of American presidential inaugural medals.

MARVIN SADIK, *Director*
National Portrait Gallery
Smithsonian Institution

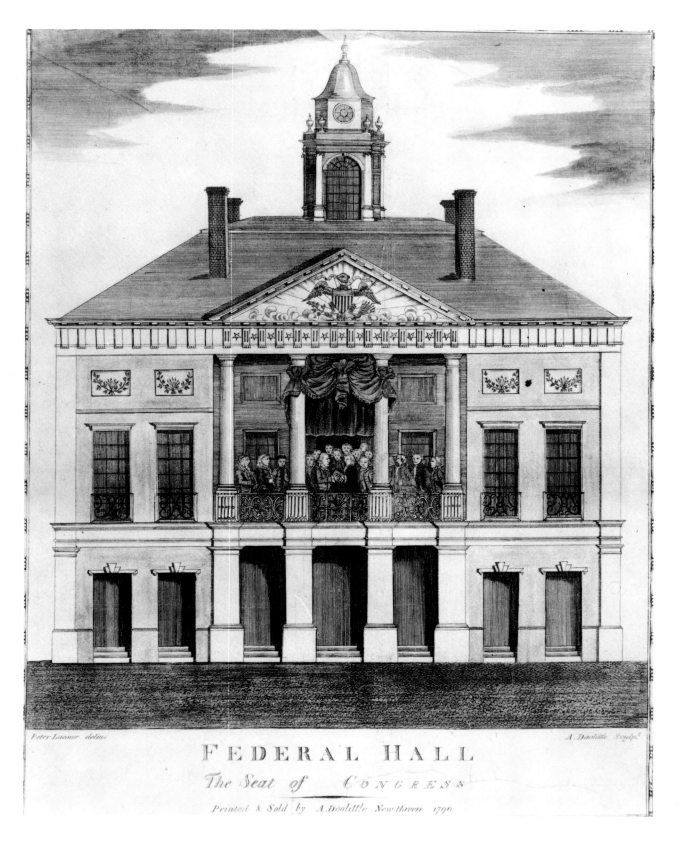

FEDERAL HALL

The Seat of Congress

Printed & Sold by A. Doolittle New Haven 1790

Federal Hall, The Seat of Congress
Amos Doolittle after a drawing by Peter Lacour
Engraving, 1790
The Historical Society of Pennsylvania

12

GEORGE
WASHINGTON
TO
ABRAHAM
LINCOLN
1789-
1861

Under the American Constitution, the President of the United States serves for a term of four years, and before entering that office, he must solemnly swear, or affirm, that he will serve faithfully and to the best of his ability preserve, protect, and defend the Constitution. From the very beginning, this oath-taking by the man chosen as President has been treated by his fellow citizens as a moment of portent in the life of the republic, a time of dedication and celebration of the essential American idea of self-government. Each such occasion has been an inauguration, an initiation of new things. By constitutional stricture, the votes of the Electoral College are counted before the assembled Congress, and the Congress notifies the President-elect that he has been chosen. Traditionally, the President-elect has taken the oath in the presence of the Congress, the representatives of the American people. This formal ceremony, conducted by the Congress, has been simplicity itself, consisting normally of little more than the oath-taking and speech by the new President.

The celebration of the inauguration, however, has been something else, normally conducted by the friends and allies of the President and the leading citizens of the capital city. Until recent years, the extent of these unofficial celebrations depended largely on the whim of the President-elect and the circumstances under which he took the oath of office. The formal ceremony of the first inauguration, held in New York City, the country's first national capital, was arranged by a joint committee of the Congress, but there were extensive celebrations of the event, sponsored by the local citizenry. George Washington was escorted to the formal ceremony by a parade under the command of Colonel Morgan Lewis, later Governor of New York. That night there was a fireworks display, and a week later, on the arrival of Martha Washington, the New Yorkers gave an inaugural ball for the new President and his lady. The parade, the fireworks, and the ball would become, in the many decades to follow, the staples of the unofficial celebrations of presidential inaugurations.

There was something else begun here that would last over the decades, and indeed take on in time the substance of a national art form. At Washington's first inauguration, there appeared special mementoes for the occasion, and Washington himself wore them. William Maclay, one of Pennsylvania's first Senators, attended this inauguration and in his journal described Washington: "He was dressed in deep brown, with metal buttons, with an eagle on them. . . ." Those buttons on Washington's broadcloth coat had been especially made for this occasion, as had the coat itself. Washington's friend Henry Knox, soon to be the first Secretary of War, had hired William Rollinson (1762–1842), an engraver, to chase the arms of the United States on a set of gilt buttons to be worn by Washington on his inauguration day. Rollinson, an Englishman, had arrived in the United States only a few weeks before, and Knox had sent samples of Rollinson's buttons to Washington, who was still at his home in Mount Vernon. Washington admired them and wrote back to Knox with a request to order more. "As it requires six more of the large (engraved) buttons to trim the coat in the manner I wish it to be," he wrote, "I would thank you, my good sir, for procuring that number and retaining them in your hands until my arrival in New York."

Once in New York, Washington had Rollinson's buttons sewn in place on his inauguration coat. Thus, at the start, Washington himself had marked this occasion with these special tokens. They were the forerunners of all the other buttons, ribbons, badges, and medals of later inaugurations of other Presidents.

In the century that followed, the official Inaugural Committee itself would evolve out of the necessity to create a group to organize systematically what were first called the "unofficial" activities inherent in the inauguration. In time, thousands of Americans would come to the national seat of government which was moved to Washington, D.C., in 1800, to attend these presidential inaugurations. They needed lodging; they needed food; they needed protection from the unscrupulous; they needed entertainment beyond the simple swearing-in ceremony conducted by the Congressional Committee of Arrangements.

In that century also, out of the American instinct for souvenirs, out of the broader human instinct to mark an important occasion with a permanent meaningful memento, the idea of special inaugural medals evolved. Sporadically, over these years, an inaugural medal would be struck for this President, or that President, but there was as yet no system to the practice. An inaugural medal was struck when it occurred to someone to strike one. They had different motives. In some few cases, an artist hoped advancement for his career. More commonly, an enterprising individual saw a chance to make some money by selling inaugural medals to the public.

At the first inauguration, in 1789, President Washington was not alone in wearing special inaugural buttons on his coat. Others in the crowd did so too, for the button manufacturers in New York and Connecticut had seen this as an opportunity to sell their wares. They produced a variety of different buttons for Washington's inauguration. Some had an eagle clasping arrows and a branch of palm leaves. Some carried the words: "Long Live the President." Others carried such legends as "Remember March Fourth, 1789," "The Majesty Of The People," "March The Fourth 1789 Memorable Era," or "E Pluribus Unum," the new nation's motto. Some carried Washington's initials, GW. Among the more popular were those depicting an unbroken chain of thirteen links, with the initials of the thirteen original states. More than two dozen types of these buttons were made, according to the researches of Alphaeus H. Albert, and not surprisingly they were treasured by the families of those who wore them on that memorable day.

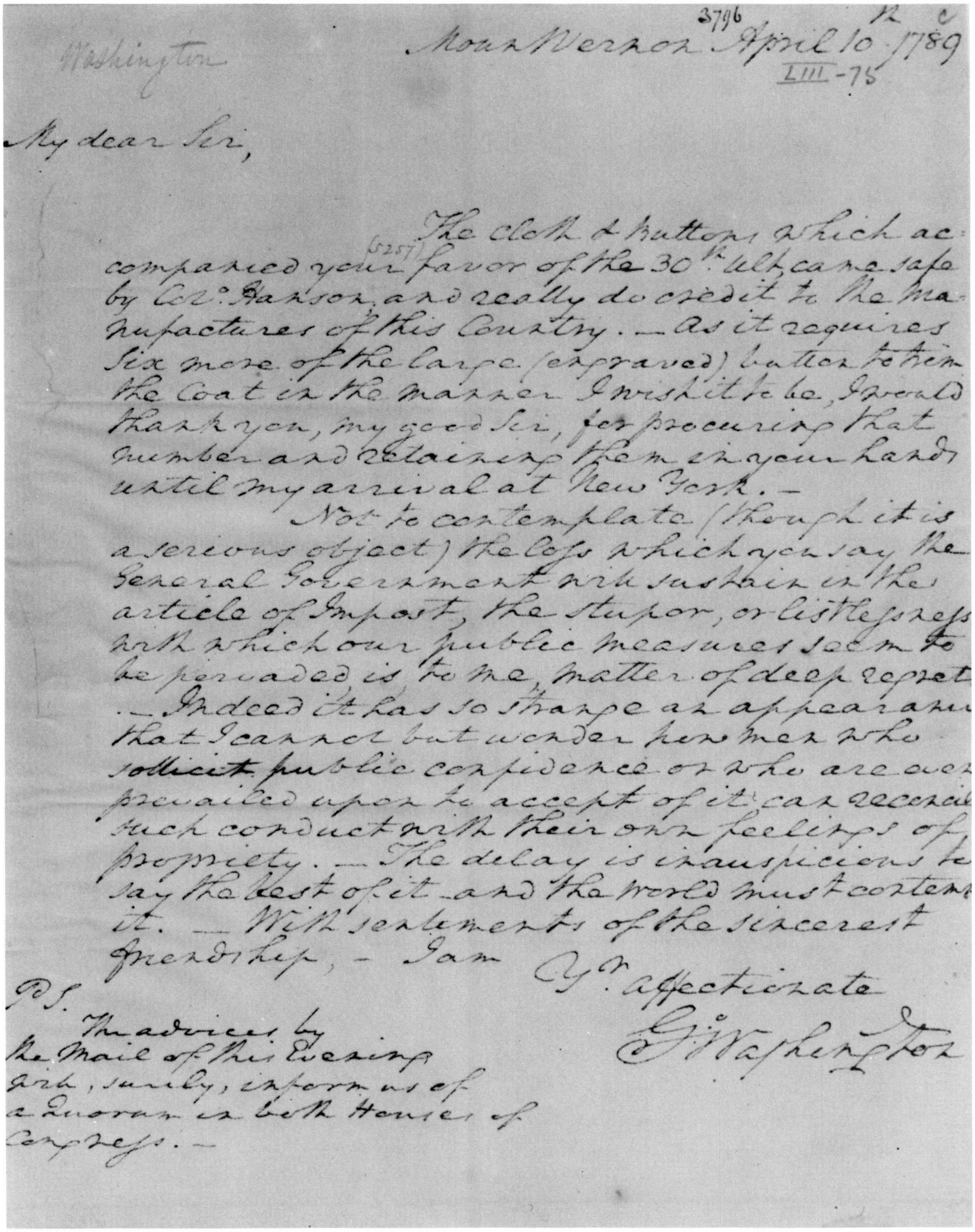

Mount Vernon April 10. 1789

My dear Sir,

The cloth & buttons which accompanied your favor of the 30th Ult, came safe by Colo. Hanson, and really do credit to the manufactures of this Country. — As it requires Six more of the large (engraved) button to trim the Coat in the manner I wish it to be, I would thank you, my good Sir, for procuring that number and retaining them in your hands until my arrival at New York. —

Not to contemplate (though it is a serious object) the loss which you say the General Government will sustain in the article of Impost, the stupor, or listlessness with which our public measures seem to be pervaded is to me, matter of deep regret. — Indeed it has so strange an appearance that I cannot but wonder how men who sollicit public confidence or who are over prevailed upon to accept of it can reconcile such conduct with their own feelings of propriety. — The delay is inauspicious to say the best of it, and the world must contemn it. — With sentiments of the sincerest friendship, — I am Yr. affectionate

G⁰ Washington

P.S. The advices by the Mail of this Evening will, surely, inform us of a quorum in both Houses of Congress. —

Letter, George Washington to Henry Knox, April 10, 1789
Massachusetts Historical Society

Eagle with date
Brass, 34 mm
Alphaeus H. Albert

"GW" with linked states border
Brass, 34 mm
Private collection

"GW" in oval center
Brass, 34 mm
Private collection

These inaugural buttons were contemporary mementoes of Washington's first inauguration, but more ambitious artistic projects to commemorate it were undertaken in the months immediately following. Especially notable was the portrait medal of Washington executed by Samuel Brooks, a Philadelphia goldsmith and seal engraver. This medal was struck and sold by Jacques Manly in early 1790 and is known historically as the "Manly medal," named for the producer rather than the artist. It was the first medal with Washington's portrait struck in the United States. Manly sold replicas of it in white metal for $1.00 each, in bronze for $2.00, in fine silver for $4.00, and in gold according to weight. On its reverse, the medal states that Washington was elected President in 1789.

Manly medal
Samuel Brooks
Silver, 48 mm
Private collection

Even as Manly was selling his medals in Philadelphia, another artist in New York was sketching George Washington as he attended services at Trinity Church. This was Joseph Wright (1756–1793), the painter, and from his crayon sketches he made an etching that was praised at the time as an excellent likeness of the President. From this etched portrait, an engraver named Twigg cut dies for a medal that also carried the legend that Washington had been elected President in 1789. Struck in white metal, this was sold to the public like the Manly medal.

Neither the Manly medal nor the Twigg medal, strictly speaking, could be called inaugural medals, but they suggested what might be done thereafter. In 1793, following Washington's second inauguration, a medal in two sizes was sold to the

Twigg medal
Twigg after Joseph Wright
White metal, 35 mm
Private collection

public. These are known as the "Success tokens" from the inscription on the reverse: "Success to the United States." J. Doyle Dewitt, in his study on American political buttons and medals, stated that these were struck to commemorate Washington's second inauguration.

No medal marked the inauguration of John Adams as President in 1797; but in that same year a medal was struck to note the retirement of Washington from the presidency. Artistically, it is an important work, designed by the celebrated die-sinker, Thomas Halliday (circa 1780–?), in England. Washington's decision not to seek or accept a third term set a national tradition as important as any other, and his retirement from the office warranted a medal as much as did his inaugurations.

Thomas Jefferson, the first President inaugurated in the city of Washington, by his own wish had the simplest of inauguration rituals, and afterwards he returned to his boardinghouse where he continued to live for another three weeks as one of the

Washington "Success" tokens
Bronze, 26 mm, 20 mm
Massachusetts Historical Society

regular roomers. Only then did he move into the President's House. For all his democratic tendencies, Jefferson was honored with an inaugural medal of striking distinction. It was the work of John Reich, a German-born die-sinker who had come to the United States in 1800 at the age of thirty-two with hopes of gainful employment. Shortly after Jefferson became President, on March 4, 1801, Reich appealed to him for help, and with his appeal he sent samples of his work. Jefferson replied with the suggestion that Reich present himself to the Director of the Mint, Elias Boudinot, in Philadelphia. Jefferson also wrote to Boudinot, asking him to use his own judgment on whether to hire Reich. "I received from a German of the name of Reich some specimens of engraving & a wish to be employed," Jefferson wrote. "He is just arrived

Halliday medal
Thomas Halliday
Bronze, 54 mm
Private collection

Jefferson mug, a souvenir of the
first inauguration in Washington, D.C.
Division of Political History,
Smithsonian Institution

Jefferson inaugural medal
John Reich
Silver, 45 mm
Massachusetts Historical Society

& in distress." Boudinot wrote back to Jefferson on June 16, 1801, that Reich had called, that he had been impressed by the samples of the man's work, and that he had set Reich to work "on a particular medal" to test his abilities further. Boudinot said he felt obliged to use "great precaution" on hiring Reich until he had good evidence of his personal integrity, no small matter for employment in the United States Mint.

Early in 1802 Jefferson received copies of a medal, made by Reich, and struck, in the words of Reich's advertisements, "to commemorate ... the auspicious day, which raised Mr. Jefferson to the dignity of President over a free people." Reich charged $4.25 for the medal in silver, $1.25 in tin. Jefferson was obviously pleased with it, and he sent copies to his daughters. "I enclose you a medal executed by an artist lately from Europe and who appears to be equal to any in the world," Jefferson wrote to his daughter Martha. "It is taken from Houdon's bust, for he never saw me."

His daughter was delighted. "I received with gratitude and pleasure inexpressible, my dearest father, the elegant medal you sent me," she replied. "It arrived safely without a scratch even, and is I think a good likeness; but as I found fault with Houdon for making you too old I shall have the same quarrel with the medal also. You have many years to live before the likeness can be a perfect one."

John Reich's advertisement in the Aurora General Advertiser, *February 17, 1802*
Library of Congress

This was the first inaugural medal.

In 1801, the United States Mint had begun striking special silver medals for presentation to appropriate Indian chiefs, who wore them as badges of special honor. Often confused with inaugural medals, these medals carried the portrait of the incumbent President on their obverse and "Peace and Friendship" on the reverse with clasped hands and crossed tomahawk and peace pipe. Similar medals had been given to the Indians by the French, the Spanish, and the British, in Jefferson's phrase, "from time immemorial." They had played an important role in the tenuous relations with the Indian tribes. The American practice of making Indian peace medals continued to the late nineteenth century, the last struck for Benjamin Harrison. They also played a part in the development of the idea of striking commemorative medals for each President's inauguration. In fact, the first of these medals struck, bearing the portrait of Jefferson, long had been attributed by the Mint itself to John Reich, the die-sinker who made Jefferson's inaugural medal. The portraits on the two medals look like they could have come from the same hand, but modern scholarship has credited the Jefferson peace medal to Robert Scot (active in Philadelphia 1781–1820), the Mint's chief engraver at that time.

19

My dear Martha   Washington Apr. 3. 1802.

I recieved Anne's letter by the last post, in which she forgot
to mention the health of the family, but I presume it good. I inclose
you a medal executed by an artist lately from Europe and who appears
to be equal to any in the world. it is taken from Houdon's bust, for he
never saw me. it sells the more readily as the prints which have been of-
-fered the public are such miserable caracatures. Congress will probably rise
within three weeks and I shall be on in a week or ten days afterwards.
my last to mr Randolph explained my expectations as to your moti-
-ons during his journey. I wrote lately to Maria, encouraging her to pay
us a flying visit at least while you are here, and proposing to mr Eppes
so to time his next plantation visit in Albemarle as to meet me there
in the beginning of May. my last information from the Hundred stated
them all well, little Francis particularly healthy. Anne writes me
that Ellen will be through all her books before I come. she may count
therefore on my bringing her a new supply. — I have desired Lilly
to make the usual provision of necessaries for me at Monticello. and
if he should be at a loss for the particulars to consult with you.
my orders as to the garden were to sow & plant as usual, and to fur-
-nish you with the proceeds. order them therefore freely: you know they
will do nothing if you leave it to their delicacy. I am looking forward
with impatience to the moment when I can embrace you in all my affection
and the dear children. it already occupies much of my thoughts as the
time approaches. present me affectionately to mr Randolph, and be
assured yourself of my tenderest love.

                                        Th: Jefferson

Mrs Randolph.

Letter, Thomas Jefferson to his daughter, Martha, April 3, 1802
The Pierpont Morgan Library

Adams Indian peace medal
Moritz Fürst
Silver, 76 mm
National Portrait Gallery, Smithsonian Institution

There can be no doubt about the next inaugural medal made or its artist. This marked the inauguration of John Quincy Adams on March 4, 1825. The Commissioner of Indian Affairs, Thomas L. McKenney, asked Moritz Fürst, a Hungarian-born die-sinker, to make the dies for the Adams Indian peace medals. Fürst had already met Adams, and Adams had agreed to his request to sit for a portrait. Adams set May 30, 1825, as the day, eight o'clock in the morning as the hour, and recorded the incident in his diary this way: *Mr. Fürst, the Medalist, came this morning and I sat to him about half an hour to make a profile of my face, with a pencil on paper from which he is to engrave it on the die for the medals to be distributed to the Indians. In about ten days the die will be so far advanced that he will ask two or three sittings more, and he is engraving a separate medal for himself, the head of which he intends to engrave in the antique costume. In the medals for the Indians the bust is in the modern dress.*

The medal Fürst was engraving for himself was an inauguration medal, which he intended to sell to the public much the way Reich had done with his medal of

Adams inaugural medal
Moritz Fürst
Silver, 51 mm
Massachusetts Historical Society

Jefferson. After Fürst had the die cut, he sent an impression from it to the President and requested an order. He wanted Adams as a patron. "I have oppen'd a subscription paper, for the purpose to collect subscribers," he wrote to Adams, "and as soon as I have obtained a suffitient number of subscribers, I shall get the Medallions coined."

Adams ordered ten of the medals in silver, and Fürst promised to select out for him the ten best of those struck. The ten best would be none too good, as far as Adams was concerned: he did not like the portrait, and he liked the artist less. "The man is pinchingly poor, both in purse and as an artist," he wrote of Fürst in his diary. Fürst repeatedly asked for his help on commissions, and Adams referred to him again: "This person is a wretched Medalist, and a half-witted man; but an untiring petitioner. . . ." Adams repeatedly had to ask for Fürst's bill, and when he got it, he was upset. Fürst charged him $10 for each of the medals; Adams believed they were worth about $1.00 each. He paid the bill, however, without questioning Fürst about it.

Not until 1833 was another inaugural medal struck, this time by the Mint's chief coiner, Adam Eckfeldt (1769–1852), to honor the second inauguration of Andrew Jackson. It was tiny, the size of a dime, and was made in gold, silver, and copper. The portrait of Jackson was strong, and the reverse carried the legend: "And. Jackson Inaugurated Presidt. U.S. Second Term Mar. IV 1833." For Jackson's first inauguration in 1829, special buttons had been made with inscriptions engraved on the inside.

Jackson inaugural button
Brass, 20 mm
Alphaeus H. Albert

Jackson inaugural medal
Gold, 18 mm
Massachusetts Historical Society

With the inauguration of Martin Van Buren in 1837, the Mint's officials found an additional use for the Indian peace medals. By changing the design on the reverse, they turned them into inaugural medals. Moritz Fürst modelled the portrait of President Van Buren, apparently from a sitting by the President for that purpose. The Mint's officials used this die to make the Indian peace medal, but they also coupled it with a different reverse, with the words "Inaugurated March 4th A.D. 1837" inscribed with an ornate wreath on the two-and-a-half-inch medal. These were struck in copper, although some were silver-plated.

For President William Henry Harrison, who died just one month after his inauguration, the United States Mint did not make an Indian peace medal. Rather, they used the portrait of his successor, John Tyler, and a remarkable portrait it was, the work of Ferdinand Pettrich (1798–1872), a German-born sculptor. For this sensitive likeness, the sculptor received only $50. Again, the Mint's officials muled this portrait, made for the Indian peace medal, with an inauguration reverse.

Van Buren inaugural medal
Moritz Fürst
Copper, 62 mm
Private collection

Curiously, they used the date April 4, 1841, the day President Harrison died, and not April 6, the day Tyler took the oath as President. The medal was two-and-a-half inches in diameter.

Again with the inauguration of James K. Polk in 1845, the Mint's officials took the occasion of making a new Indian peace medal to produce an inaugural medal. The portrait of President Polk, in startlingly bold relief, is the work of John Gadsby Chapman, an American artist who had studied in Italy and was better known for his paintings than his sculpture. According to R. W. Julian, the outstanding scholar of Mint medals, the Mint's chief engraver, Franklin Peale, struck six of these Polk inaugural medals in copper and then had them gilded to present to President Polk and his party on an official visit to the Mint on June 24, 1847. The cost for the six medals and their presentation cases was $17.

Still another presidential inaugural medal was made by the Mint from the peace medal prepared for the administration of Zachary Taylor. The portrait was the work of Henry Kirke Brown (1814–1886), a major mid-nineteenth-century American portrait sculptor.

Tyler inaugural medal
Ferdinand Pettrich
Copper, 62 mm
Private collection

Polk inaugural medal
John Gadsby Chapman
Copper, 62 mm
Private collection

Taylor inaugural medal
Henry Kirke Brown
Copper, 62 mm
Richard B. Dusterberg

The inaugural medals made only in the two-and-a-half-inch size by the Mint for Presidents Van Buren, Tyler, Polk, and Taylor, were apparently sold by the Mint's officials for their own private profit, even though the work of producing them was done by government employees with government facilities. The Mint's chief engravers contracted with private parties for medals as early as the 1820s and kept the profits for themselves. By the 1840s, this amounted to a notorious scandal, which was not ended until President Franklin Pierce summarily fired Franklin Peale as chief engraver in 1853. After the one of Zachary Taylor, no more inaugural medals were made with peace medal portraits.

Although the Mint had made no Indian peace medal for President William Henry Harrison, his inauguration in 1841 had been marked by the striking of several private medals and a ribbon. One of the medals warrants special note: the reverse carried the words "Inauguration Medal Capital March 4, 1841."

The inauguration of Franklin Pierce
Wood engraving, in the Illustrated News, *March 12, 1853*
Library of Congress

In 1857, a handsome medal was struck, in white metal, to commemorate the inauguration of James Buchanan as President, and one medal only marks Abraham Lincoln's first inauguration. It probably was made some time afterward.

Harrison inaugural medal
White metal, 36 mm
The American Numismatic Society, New York

25

Buchanan inaugural medal
White metal, 60 mm
University of Hartford Collection

Over these years, before the Civil War, the celebrations of each succeeding President's inauguration had become more complex. Jefferson had wanted no display, and he had received little. President Madison's wife Dolly had different ideas; it was she who revived the inaugural ball in 1809. Dolly Madison was the belle of that ball, for certain, but the new President was miserable with the discomfiture of the crowded room. "I would much rather be in bed," he said at the time, and left as soon as he could. Significantly, that ball was sponsored by a special committee of managers, composed of twelve of the most prominent citizens of Washington. Significantly also, admission was by purchase ticket, not invitation. The ball managers needed funds to pay for the hall in Long's Hotel, the decorations, and the supper.

For the inaugurations that followed, similar balls were sponsored by similar committees of managers. Gradually, the sponsoring groups became larger and included some of the most famous members of the Senate and House of Representatives. In 1837, every effort was made to outdo all previous inaugural balls. "The managers were gentlemen of high official rank and young men of fashion," a contemporary wrote. "The indication of their rank was a piece of white ribbon, decorating the lapel of their coats." In 1841, the renowned Daniel Webster headed the list of managers for the year's ball, and for the one in 1845, the managers included James Buchanan and Stephen A. Douglas.

While the inaugural ball became organized and even standardized, the other activities had no central operation, and there were continued responsibilities not met. In 1829, at the first inauguration of Andrew Jackson as President, many thousands of persons came to Washington to attend the ceremonies. "Where the multitude slumbered last night is inconceivable," a contemporary wrote, "unless it were on their mother earth, curtained by the unbroken sky." Because Jackson's wife had but recently died, there was no ball, but Jackson did hold a reception at the White House, which turned into a near riot. Jackson himself escaped injury only because he was physically rescued from the crush of the crowd. "What a pity! What a pity!" one witness to the chaos cried. "No arrangements had been made, no police officers placed on duty and the whole house had been inundated by the rabble mob."

The first known photograph of an inauguration. On March 4, 1857, when James Buchanan took the presidential oath, the Senate Wing of the Capitol was not yet completed.
Photograph courtesy Division of Political History,
Smithsonian Institution

No arrangements had been made, no arrangements to house and feed the thousands who had come to Washington, no arrangements to protect the public safety nor even the safety of the President himself. Those running the balls, inauguration after inauguration, did develop a workable plan of operations, and they were able to raise funds enough to repay their costs. They provided an example of how to run an inaugural affair, and in time their committees of managers would be expanded into a citizens' committee to take care of all the varied activities involved in celebrating a President's inauguration. That did not come until after the Civil War, and when the time came, those committees would by their own operations develop still another inaugural tradition, like those of the ball, the parade, and the fireworks. That would be the tradition of striking an inaugural medal, in gold, for the President, as a memento for him. It was this tradition, long in the making, which had its start in those special bronze buttons chased with the arms of the United States that George Washington wore on his inaugural coat in 1789.

Invitation to the 1841 inaugural ball
Private collection

President's Levee, or all Creation going to the White House, Washington
Robert Cruikshank
Aquatint, in The Playfair Papers, or: Brother Jonathan,
the Smartest Nation in all Creation, *London, 1841*

ABRAHAM
LINCOLN
TO
GROVER
CLEVELAND
1861-
1885

In the years up to the Civil War, despite the haphazard manner of celebrating presidential inaugurations, certain traditions had evolved to the point where they were automatically expected. For example, simple safety suggested that the parade be cancelled in 1861, at Abraham Lincoln's first inauguration, with the country on the verge of civil strife. Lincoln himself was worried. "Don't let your wife come to my inauguration," he advised a friend. "It is best for our women to remain indoors on that day, as the bullets may be flying." For all that, the inaugural parade was held, if heavily guarded by military units, and so was a ball that night. Tradition proved stronger than the fears of assassination. Not even in this year of crisis did those in Washington act to place all the varied inauguration activities under one central command. One group of Washingtonians sponsored the ball, another group organized the parade. And there were needs, increasingly obvious now, to which those dealing with the inaugurations had not yet addressed themselves. For one, substantial sums of money were needed to finance these celebrations, and no clear system of raising them had been devised, other than the tickets sold for the inaugural ball. For another, prominent leaders from all over the country came for these functions, and courtesy required that some formal attentions be shown them. For still another, the thousands of citizens who came to Washington on their own needed help in finding a place to stay for the night and protection from any price-gouging by the Washington merchants and innkeepers.

In 1865, for the first time, an attempt was made to organize the celebrations in a systematic way under one command. The Washingtonians created the General Inaugural Committee to oversee all the activities other than the swearing-in of Lincoln for his second term. Named chairman of the new committee was Lewis Clephane, a prominent Washingtonian who had been postmaster at one period, newspaper publisher at another. Records for this committee are scant, but Clephane apparently was appointed because of his strenuous labors in the cause of Lincoln's Republican party. In 1854, he had been co-founder of the Republican Party in Washington, D.C. In 1864, he had organized and chaired a special committee to help reelect Lincoln.

Serving under Clephane, as chairman of the inaugural ball committee, was Benjamin B. French, another prominent Washingtonian who in 1861 had been grand marshal of the inaugural parade. This year, also serving under Clephane, was the grand marshal of the parade, Daniel Reaves Goodloe, a journalist and friend of Lincoln.

The General Inaugural Committee itself was composed of Republican partisans, from Washington primarily, and its operations proved something less than entirely successful. The parade passed without incident, other than that this was the first such parade to include Negroes freed by the war not yet over. The trouble came at the inaugural ball. The committee had sold tickets at $10 each, the price to include an elegant midnight supper. Whatever profits resulted were to go to the needy families of Civil War soldiers. When supper was announced, there were inadequate facilities to seat the thousands, and a near riot followed. Impatient guests grabbed whole chickens, halves of turkeys, legs of veal; many were drunk and smashed glasses and china without let. It was a shocking, unpleasant end to an inauguration celebration, and members of Congress would remember it when asked in the future to help an Inaugural Committee solve its problems. It was an inauspicious start for the first formal Inaugural Committee of Washington citizens, but it was a start. From this time on, these celebrations would always be under the charge of similar citizens' committees, and from these committees would come the tradition, not yet begun in 1865, to strike inaugural medals to mark these occasions.

In 1869, the Republican National Committee assumed the responsibility for appointing the Inaugural Committee, this time entitled "The General Committee on Unofficial Inauguration Ceremonies." Named chairman was Robert C. Schenck, a respected Congressman from Ohio, also known as an authority on draw poker. Other members were General William T. Sherman of Civil War fame, the mayors of Washington and Georgetown, and Washington businessmen and journalists. The General Committee created, for the first time, an executive committee to control actual operations, and the executive committee met January 27, 1869, and passed a resolution requesting permission from Congress to hold President Grant's inaugural ball in the Capital's great rotunda. That request prompted a Senate debate in which the drunkenness at the 1865 ball was not forgotten. "If there is to be a ball," stated Senator Simon Cameron of Pennsylvania, "let it be given by the people of the city. Do not let us give it an official character." The General Committee on Unofficial Inauguration Ceremonies had to look elsewhere.

Neither the 1865 nor the 1869 committees had done more, in terms of the evolutionary process from which inaugural medals would eventually emerge, than to advance their own organizational development. In 1865, two tiny, somewhat non-descript medals had been struck for President Lincoln's second inauguration, and four years later, William H. Key, the Philadelphian who was assistant engraver at the United States Mint and a private die-sinker, had executed a handsome medal for Grant's inauguration. These were private ventures, and it would be years yet before an Inaugural Committee would authorize its own souvenirs.

In 1873, under the command and control of an extraordinary man, Alexander R. Shepherd, the Inaugural Committee took its modern form. There would be changes, modifications, and expansions in the years to come, but the committee created by Shepherd for President Grant's second inauguration would serve as the model. Shepherd, a local businessman turned municipal reformer, had taken charge of Washington under legislation voted by Congress in 1871, and turned a squalid town with unpaved streets and open sewers into a modern city. He similarly modern-

Lincoln inaugural medals
Silver, 18 mm
Private collection

Lincoln medal
Silver, 19 mm
Private collection

Grant inaugural medal
William H. Key
White metal, 50 mm
Private collection

ized the Inaugural Committee, this year called "Committee of Arrangements, Presidential Inauguration, March 4, 1873," of which he was president. He set up its headquarters at 17th Street and Pennsylvania Avenue, scarcely a block from the White House, and directed the entire inaugural celebration. He created nine subsidiary committees, giving each special responsibilities that ranged from sponsoring the ball to negotiating with the railroads for special trains and rates for anyone who wanted to come to Washington for the occasion. Especially important, he created a committee on finance, for the first time placing there control and responsibility over the inauguration's increasingly complex finances.

Shepherd issued a broadside to the nation, cordially inviting citizens everywhere to come to Washington for President Grant's second inauguration, and stating that he wished this celebration to be "worthy of the man and the great nation that has again selected him to preside over its destinies." He announced: *The committees appointed by the citizens of the metropolis are making extensive arrangements for the entertainment of visitors, and will do all in their power to render them as comfortable as the means under their control will allow. The public halls and all other apartments that can be obtained will be engaged for the accommodation of organized bodies.*

In addition to the ceremonies at the Capitol, there will be a civic and military procession, fireworks, illuminations, and a grand ball in the immense building . . . now being erected for the purpose.

Committee President Shepherd, in short, created a complex Inaugural Committee to operate an extensive celebration and then invited the country to attend.

To the White House, March 4, 1869
(Ulysses S. Grant and Schuyler Colfax)
Auguste Peyrau
Bronze statuette
Museum of Fine Arts, Boston, M. & M. Karolik Collection

Of course, he had to depend on volunteers to carry out the various chores necessary to a successful operation, and there were so many different functions, and so many performing them, that this committee for the first time issued badges. There are few records extant, but these badges seem to have been primarily, if not solely, for identification purposes. Years before, at the inauguration of Martin Van Buren in 1837, those in charge of the ball had worn white identifying ribbons in their lapels. In 1841, private hands had produced an inaugural ribbon in silk, stamped with Harrison's portrait and the inaugural date, and these were obviously sold at the event. In 1849, for the inauguration of President Zachary Taylor, a somewhat similar silk ribbon had been sold; it had a stamped portrait of the President and a facsimile of his autograph. The 1873 committee apparently did not issue its badges as souvenirs, but purely for identification, and they probably were no more than colored ribbons. Those on the reception committee received white badges; those on the ball committee badges of red, white, and blue. The chairman of the inaugural ball had a gold-ribbon badge, his assistants badges of blue. Doubtlessly, there was an element of official pride in the wearing of these that went beyond mere identification, but no one could have predicted that within a few inaugurations they would develop a new tradition.

33

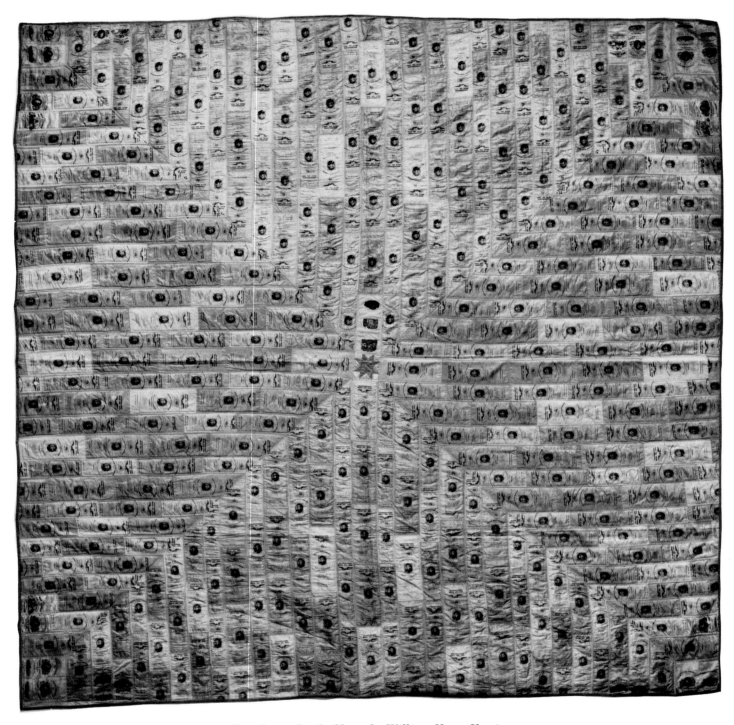

Coverlet made of ribbons for William Henry Harrison
Division of Political History, Smithsonian Institution

*Detail from coverlet showing the only known
William Henry Harrison inaugural ribbon*

*Taylor inaugural ribbon
Private collection*

The Inaugural Committee of 1877 had little to do. The presidential election had resulted essentially in a stalemate. Congress created a constitutionally questionable commission to resolve the crisis, and, after much controversy and bitterness, Rutherford B. Hayes was declared elected, just days before March 4, 1877. The inauguration was less than a joyous holiday. Many feared violence. There was an abbreviated parade, but no ball.

The Inaugural Committee in 1881, the year of James A. Garfield, called itself the "Executive Committee on Inaugural Ceremonies," and it copied much from the 1873 committee, including its subcommittee structure. John W. Thompson, the chairman, had served on Alexander Shepherd's General Managing Committee in 1873, and he was thoroughly familiar with the system that Shepherd had then initiated. He expanded on what had been done before, including the number and scope of the subsidiary committees, and he devised a technique, used ever afterwards, to generate advance funds for the Inaugural Committee. The members of the finance committee solicited money from local citizens and companies in advance of the inauguration, to give the Inaugural Committee fiscal flexibility, and pledged to repay the subscribed amounts out of revenues received from the ball. The money was placed in what was then called the Inaugural Fund. In later years, this would be called the Guarantee Fund.

The finance committee thus raised about $20,000 in advance money, and that money enabled the Inaugural Committee to do such pleasant things as order special badges for the volunteers. The inauguration, not surprisingly, proved a financial success, and each of the subscribers to the Inaugural Fund was repaid in full.

The badges ordered by the committee were meant this time for more than mere identification. The committee had arranged that they be made attractive enough to serve as souvenirs of the occasion. The ribbon of the badge was silk, and on each was imprinted, in gold lettering, a handsomely embossed seal. Beneath the date on each ribbon came the name of the particular committee for which this badge was made. Each committee was given a different-colored ribbon. Those on the executive committee received badges of royal purple; those on the decoration committee, badges of green; those on the ticket committee, badges of yellow; those on the committee of public comfort, badges of blue. This committee had created a memento. Those that followed would do the same.

In 1884, for the first time since the Civil War, the voters elected a Democrat as President, Grover Cleveland of New York, and therefore it fell to the Democratic National Committee to arrange for his inauguration on March 4, 1885. The Democrats appointed fifty citizens as the Inaugural Committee, with James G. Berret as chairman, and they chose an executive committee of fifteen to take actual charge of the celebration. The finance committee raised a Guarantee Fund of $22,000, all of which was repaid. The executive committee created no less than twenty-two subsidiary committees, including, for the first time, a special committee on inaugural badges with James P. Willet as chairman. Obviously, the inaugural badges made for the members of the 1881 Inaugural Committee had proved popular. The 1885 committee had the chore of providing equally distinctive badges, and those they made resembled the badges of 1881.

For the first time, this Inaugural Committee issued an official program, and after the ceremonies, for the first time, they published a final report on their activities. There, the committee on badges received praise for its work in providing "distinguishing" mementoes. "This duty was discharged with good taste," the report

Official Garfield inaugural badge
Private collection

Official Cleveland inaugural badge
Private collection

stated, "and the series of badges were remarkable for their beauty and fitness."

Another dimension had been added to the celebration, but the Inaugural Committees of 1881 and 1885 were not alone in producing distinctive souvenirs. In those years, private firms had entered the field. William H. Key of Philadelphia, who had made a medal for the first Grant inauguration, made another in 1881 for Garfield. So did George T. Morgan (1845–1925), also of Philadelphia, and, like Key, an engraver at the United States Mint. Key sold his medal by itself and also as the fob on a red-white-and-blue-ribboned badge. Still another smaller medal was produced for Garfield's inauguration, and it reminded its buyers that the new President had once been a canal boy. One private firm made a handsome medal for Cleveland's inauguration in 1885 that had separate portraits of the President and his Vice President on the obverse and an eagle, with a scroll in its beak, inscribed "E Pluribus Unum" on the reverse. To mark the same event, another private company made a smaller medal. Measuring only fifteen-sixteenths of an inch in diameter, the reverse carried Cleveland's famous dictum: "Public Office A Public Trust."

For both the 1881 and 1885 inaugurations, private companies also made badges, mostly for sale at the inauguration. The members of Tammany Hall, the oldest of New York Democratic clubs, however, had their own distinctive badge for Cleveland's first inauguration in 1885, but it was not as spectacular as their badge for Cleveland's second inauguration in 1893.

Garfield inaugural medal
George T. Morgan
Bronze, 38 mm
Private collection

Garfield inaugural badge
William H. Key
White metal, 33 mm
University of Hartford Collection

Garfield inaugural medal
Bronze, 25 mm
Private collection

Cleveland–Hendricks inaugural medal
White metal, 35 mm
Private collection

Cleveland inaugural medal
Copper, 24 mm
Private collection

Tammany Hall inaugural badge
Private collection

BENJAMIN HARRISON TO WILLIAM MC KINLEY

1889- 1897

After a full century, the formal inauguration of the President and the celebration that went with it had become formalized in almost predictable fashion. The Congress, of course, conducted the actual oath-taking, as it always had; but the inaugural celebration by now had grown into an immense operation, requiring systematic and organized control. From haphazard beginnings and individual initiatives, the citizens of Washington had taken that responsibility for themselves in the now fully developed concept of the official Inaugural Committee. At first, this committee tended to be composed of partisans of the President-elect, but in later years the citizens of Washington came to regard the inauguration as a civic, rather than as a partisan, obligation. By 1889, the committee members had more than traditions, like the ball and the parade, to uphold; they had also the means of doing so. On March 2, 1889, an article in the *Evening Star* of Washington explained the local citizens' role: *There is no government appropriation to defray the expenses of the inauguration. Voluntary subscriptions from private citizens furnish the means which insure a suitable and appropriate demonstration. The display of fireworks at night and the great ball, held in a magnificently decorated ballroom, form a fitting close to a memorable day.*

Without the active co-operation of the citizens the grand procession would probably be an insignificant marshalling of a few military companies and civic associations. By means of an admirable system committees of citizens devote time and labor in corresponding with organizations throughout the country. They provide suitable quarters for them in this city at moderate prices and receive them on their arrival, and see that they are cared for. All the innumerable details of an affair of this magnitude are carefully considered months beforehand.

This was a far cry from the first inauguration held in Washington, when President Jefferson walked back to his boardinghouse after taking the oath. The critical point in the Inaugural Committee's operation had been its finances. Without adequate funds, the committee could not function properly. Without adequate funds, it could not provide such pleasantries as the inaugural badges already made for the

*April 29, 1889, naval parade and reenactment of George Washington's arrival in New York City
for the first inauguration. President Benjamin Harrison rides in the boat in the foreground.
Reproduced in* The History of the Centennial Celebration, *New York, 1892*

1881 and 1885 committee members. With the funds now available, the Inaugural Committee could undertake even more ambitious projects than it had in the past, and for the inauguration of Benjamin Harrison in 1889, it did just that. For this inauguration and for those in 1893 and 1897, the committees authorized badges which, beyond providing identification, had another significance: attached to them were inaugural medals.

In 1889, the United States actually celebrated two presidential inaugurations. The first, on March 4 in Washington, celebrated Benjamin Harrison as the twenty-third President of the United States. The second, on April 30 in New York City, celebrated the one-hundredth anniversary of the swearing-in of George Washington as the first President. President Harrison, of course, attended the New York ceremony.

Both occasions prompted an outpouring of souvenir materials from private companies, notably in the field of badges and medals. The New York celebration received greater attention from dealers, but the committee in charge took an extraordinary action on its own: it commissioned Augustus Saint-Gaudens, the renowned sculptor, to design a special medal honoring George Washington. Saint-Gaudens declined a fee, but he agreed to design a medal which an assistant, Philip Martiny (1856–1927), executed. Saint-Gaudens had long admired the Renaissance medalists, notably Antonio Pisano, called Pisanello, and he drew his design in the manner of that artist. Cast by the Gorham Company of New York, this medal was sold, by the authority of the committee, to the public. The New York committee did something

41

more: it contracted with the Tiffany Company to make, for its members, a ceremonial badge, using a smaller version of the Saint-Gaudens design. The idea of a badge with attached medal, of course, was not new. A private firm had made such a badge for the Garfield inauguration, and in Washington, even as Martiny was completing Saint-Gauden's design, other private companies were making similar badges.

The Washington committee, charged with arranging the celebration of Harrison's inauguration on March 4, had been duly created. The Republican National Chairman, Matthew Quay, named a Washington lawyer, Alexander T. Britton, as chairman, and Britton followed the previous practice of establishing the various committees to raise funds, sponsor the ball, organize the parade, care for the out-of-towners, and so on. Britton appointed an eleven-man committee on badges, under the chairmanship of Simon Wolf, also a Washington lawyer, with instructions to provide appropriate badges for all committee members and volunteers working on the inauguration. Thus, according to the *Washington Star,* "the members of the various committees might be properly designated and thus enabled to discharge their duties in a proper manner."

Chairman Wolf and his committee members had more than that in mind. They had to arrange for badges that would meet general approval, especially after the popularity of the badges produced in 1881 and 1885. By late January, 1889, the committee had let a contract to produce 1,600 badges for Inaugural Committee members. For these, the committee agreed to pay $1,337, a substantial amount, especially when compared to what had been spent in previous years. The expense suggests that the committee members had contracted for more costly badges than ever before. Their responsibility, as they themselves saw it, was "to obtain a badge to designate the members of the various committees, which should be original, of artistic design, and embracing features that would properly typify the occasion." This was the centennial inauguration, a century since Washington had taken the oath, and that was an obvious matter to consider for the design.

The badges won praise from the Harrison Inaugural Committee in its final report: "How well they succeeded is evidenced by the extraordinary demand made for the badge adopted, which was of novel and attractive design, and will be cherished by the possessor as a valuable memento of the centennial inauguration."

Unfortunately, the surviving records do not specify the terms of the contract nor even the name of the firm which made these inaugural badges. Only one type of inaugural badge extant, however, seems to meet the known requirements for markings to show the wearer's committee assignment. Made by the Wm. Friederich Company of Washington, D. C., this badge consists of a medal, suspended from two bars, on a red, white, and blue ribbon. Small silk ribbons between the "Centennial" and "Inauguration" suspension bars had, stamped in gold, the name of the specific subsidiary inaugural committee to which the wearer was assigned: the committee on "Public Comfort," the "Floor" committee for the inaugural ball, and so on. This would seem the critical point: these badges carried the names of the various subsidiary and functioning committees of the Harrison Inaugural Committee. There could have been no purpose for these identifying cross-ribbons other than to identify members of the various committees.

The medals on these badges were struck in various metals, the most common being white metal. Some were silvered; some were bronzed. At least one was struck in gold, presumably as a formal presentation piece. Moreover, the price paid by the Inaugural Committee, $1,337 for an announced 1,600 badges, would indicate badges of the quality made by the Friederich Company. The committee must have received more expensive badges than those of 1881 and 1885 without medals. Had the 1889 committee purchased a badge without a medal, the price would have been less than one-eighth of the price actually paid. As late as 1909, an Inaugural Committee would be able to buy 3,800 identity ribbon badges, without medals, for only $367. The style and size of the 1889 badge were consistent with the official badges of the inaugurations immediately following, 1893 and 1897. The price paid for the 1889 badges was also consistent with the prices paid for similarly medaled, official inaugural badges in 1893 and 1897.

The difficulty with identifying the Friederich Company badge as definitely the one ordered by the committee is that the company made slightly variant versions of the piece, which were offered for sale at both celebrations, in Washington and New York. These badges did not carry the cross-ribbons identifying the committees, and they had other differences too. What appears to have happened is that the committee on badges ordered this medaled badge from the Friederich Company in January 1889. It did carry the identity cross-ribbons, and the red, white, and blue ribbon was stamped on the reverse with the company's name and location. If they were popular enough to create the demand reported by the inaugural executive committee, there must have been pressure to make them available to the public. Belatedly, the Friederich Company applied for a patent on its badge in February and stamped an announcement of this application on the badges sold in Washington and New York City. The announcement does not appear on the badges carrying the identity cross-ribbons. The obvious reason for seeking a patent was that it had become a valuable commercial item; when only the Inaugural Committee had ordered them, there seemed no need for legal protection. The Friederich Company also sold these medals suspended from eagle pin clasps.

The medal on the badge sold in New York City differed from the one sold in Washington. In New York, the portrait of George Washington was treated as the obverse of the medal, and around the Washington portrait the manufacturer added this inscription: "Geo. Washington First President Of The U.S."

Still another inaugural badge, with suspended medal, produced for the Harrison inauguration, has to be included here. This was apparently authorized by the Grand Marshal of the inaugural parade, General James A. Beaver.

General Beaver was familiar with badges and medals, and with inaugurations. In 1885, he had led a division in the inaugural parade for President Cleveland. In 1882, he had run unsuccessfully for Governor of Pennsylvania, and for that campaign he had ordered a badge with a medal portraying himself as war hero: he had lost a leg in the Civil War at the battle of Reams Station. In 1886, he again ran for Governor, this time winning, and for his inauguration, on January 18, 1887, he had his own badge, with a medallic portrait of himself. There seems no reason to doubt that Beaver assumed that his command of the Harrison inaugural parade warranted another badge and medal commemorating his role. A medal manufacturer would scarcely have produced such a medal and badge on its own initiative, giving such credit to General Beaver. The general was a wealthy man, with a lucrative law practice and ownership of a factory as well. He probably had these badges made as souvenirs for his friends and colleagues who paraded with him down Pennsylvania Avenue from the Capitol to the White House on President Harrison's inauguration day. They were made with two different types of ribbons.

The Inaugural Committee for 1893 took its cues from the 1889 committee, and

Washington inauguration centennial medal
Augustus Saint-Gaudens and Philip Martiny
Bronze, 115 mm
Private collection

Washington inauguration centennial general committee badge
Bronze, 35 mm
Private collection

Harrison–Morton committee on public comfort inaugural badge
White metal, 38 mm
Private collection

Harrison–Beaver inaugural badge
Bronze, 38 mm
Private collection

in this year there could be no doubt about inaugural badges authorized by the committee on badges. In the 1892 election, Grover Cleveland won a second term as President by defeating Benjamin Harrison. This victory pleased the Democrats even more than Cleveland's election in 1884, and they planned a grander inauguration than ever before. Their enthusiasm became too extravagant, and Cleveland himself had to call a halt to some of the proposed activities. For example, those in charge arranged for Cleveland to ride to the White House from the Capitol ceremony in a magnificently ornate carriage. The President-elect read about the plan in a newspaper. "I certainly will not ride from the Capitol to the White House in any such foolish style," he wrote to the Inaugural Committee. The committee planned a series of concerts of "sacred" music for the day after inauguration day, March 5, which was a Sunday. Clerical busybodies raised a storm, and Cleveland cancelled that plan too.

While he was at it, Cleveland wrote again to the Inaugural Committee. He had remembered his first inauguration in 1885 and what he regarded then as the shabby treatment given members of his own family. "Eight years ago," he wrote, "not a single member of my family could get within *sight or hearing* of the Inaugural Ceremonies." He wanted better tickets for them this time.

For all that, the inauguration proved a time of celebration, not recrimination. The Democratic national chairman, W. F. Harrity, again appointed James G. Berret as chairman of the General Inaugural Committee, which appointed a twenty-one-member executive committee to manage the celebration. Its chairman, James L. Norris, a Washington patent attorney, appointed the chairmen of the subsidiary committees. These groups solicited help from literally thousands of Washingtonians. The finance committee, with 240 members, raised a Guarantee Fund of $35,000. The

General Beaver gubernatorial campaign medal, 1882
White metal, 25 mm
Private collection

General Beaver gubernatorial inaugural medal, 1887
White metal, 34 mm
Private collection

reception committee included the Chief Justice of the United States, his fellow justices, many additional judges, senators, and congressmen from every state; and more than 650 others. No longer were these inaugural ceremonies in the hands of a few persons.

One of the few small committees was the one on badges with seventeen members, this year under the chairmanship of Dominic I. Murphy. They were asked to devise "appropriate badges" as identification but also as souvenirs for those volunteering their work. In the somewhat pompous, bombastic language of the Inaugural Committee in its final report, these badges "should ever remain to their possessors the cherished souvenirs of the memorable occasion."

The committee on badges negotiated a contract with the Whitehead & Hoag Company of Newark, New Jersey. Begun in 1870, this firm claimed to be "the largest

Cleveland–Stevenson executive committee inaugural badge
Silver-plated, 42 mm
Private collection

exclusive badge business in the world." The committee agreed to pay the firm $1,681.75 under a contract which provided for 4,132 committee badges, 500 for the press, and 150 for messengers. The principal badges—the most costly—were similar to those of 1889. They had medals, suspended by a red, white, and blue ribbon from a hanger which carried the inaugural date and the word "Inauguration."

The medals on these badges, struck in white metal, came in two varieties. Those for the twenty-one members of the executive committee were silvered, as a mark of prestige. Those for the other committees were bronzed.

How many of the badges included these medals can only be a matter of conjecture. Most of them did not: they were just silk ribbons stamped for the committee involved, and using the same hanger as the badges with medals. Obviously, the committee hesitated to provide everyone with the more expensive badges. The badges with medals are rarely encountered in the numismatic world, which suggests that only a few hundred of them were made.

48

Cleveland–Stevenson reception committee inaugural badge
Private collection

In 1897, the Inaugural Committee followed almost identically the procedures and practices of the committees of 1889 and 1893. The previous November, the people had elected William McKinley as President. Republican National Chairman Mark Hanna named Charles E. Bell as Chairman of the Inaugural Committee. Bell ran the celebration through the now usual executive committee, this time numbering forty-three members, and the usual subsidiary committees. John W. Thompson, chairman of the 1881 Inaugural Committee, chaired this year's finance committee and raised a Guarantee Fund of more than $47,000. James G. Berret, who had been chairman of the 1885 and 1893 Inaugural Committees, served this year on the executive committee. Simon Wolf, who had been chairman of the committee on badges in 1889, was again named to that post. Plainly, a sense of continuity had developed.

Wolf was fully familiar with the requirements for inaugural badges, and his committee awarded the contract to the Joseph K. Davison Company of Philadelphia,

McKinley–Hobart executive committee inaugural badge
Silver-plated, 44 mm
Private collection

Hawk Club, Princeton University, inaugural badge
Private collection

a commercial firm making medals and badges. The badges produced were similar
to those ordered for 1889 and 1893, and they had inaugural medals attached.

"The design selected was unique and singularly appropriate to the occasion,"
the Inaugural Committee said of the badge in its final report. "It has been in great
demand, but as the supply was limited, only those performing duty and thereby
earning it were made possessors. The committee is fully deserving of the many
congratulations it received for its good work."

How many of these badges were made, the records do not recount. In quality,
they were an improvement on those made in 1889 and 1893. The 1897 medals and
the two hangers of the badge were struck in bronze, which was more expensive than

the white metal used on the earlier badges. The committee paid $2,025 for these badges, suggesting that perhaps as many as 3,000 were produced.

The committee on badges, with the authority of the executive committee, had the Davison Company prepare three special badges, with the medals on each struck in "pure gold." The first of these was presented to President McKinley. This was the start of a new tradition. The concept of the inaugural badge had been changed. At first, it had been used merely for identification, then as a memento, a souvenir of the occasion. Now the badge had become identified not just with the Inaugural Committee, but with the President himself.

The two other badges with gold medals were given·to Vice President Hobart and Charles E. Bell, the Chairman of the Inaugural Committee.

This year also, as in 1893, the committee on badges had special badges made for the forty-three members of the executive committee. They were identical to the regular badges, except that, like the ones in 1893, the medals and hangers were silver-plated. The executive committee members held the greatest responsibilities, and their badges were intended to denote that.

In these years and the years to come, private firms found a lucrative market in the sale of inaugural tokens and badges. Some actively solicited this business. For example, the Whitehead & Hoag Company wrote to the president of the Hawk Club at Princeton University on February 9, 1897, to offer special badges to the club's members planning to attend McKinley's inauguration: *We will furnish you these at the special rate of 50 cents each, and will allow you our trade discount of 20%, making the net cost 40 cents each. If design is not entirely satisfactory, we shall be pleased to have your instructions.*

BH	1889	1	gold	(38 mm)	unknown
BH	1889	2	silver	(38 mm)	unknown
BH	1889	3	white metal	(38 mm)	unknown
BH	1889	4	bronze (Beaver)	(38 mm)	unknown

| GC | 1893 | 1 | white metal, silvered | (42 mm) | 21 |
| GC | 1893 | 2 | white metal, bronzed | (42 mm) | several hundred |

WMcK	1897	1	gold	(44 mm)	3
WMcK	1897	2	copper, silvered	(44 mm)	43
WMcK	1897	3	bronze	(44 mm)	possibly 3,000

WILLIAM
MCKINLEY
1901

In 1900, President William McKinley won reelection. Vice President Hobart had died in 1899, and Theodore Roosevelt was elected to that post. Roosevelt had been Assistant Secretary of the Navy at the outbreak of the Spanish–American War in 1898. He had resigned to volunteer for the invasion of Cuba, and there he won a fame on San Juan Hill that brought him, first, the governorship of New York, and, now, the vice presidency. The United States had won fame of its own by smashing the Spanish forces in the Caribbean and the Philippines. The United States suddenly had become a world power, and the jingoism that had propelled this country into war carried on into the inauguration of 1901. This would be the largest, most expensive inauguration ever, to befit the status of the President as a world leader.

The citizens of Washington, who long had operated the inaugural celebrations, took pride in that fact now, especially, and a statement in this year's *Official Inaugural Program* put it bluntly: "The citizens of Washington have arranged for and provided all the pomp and circumstance that has marked these occasions." There would be pomp and circumstance at this inauguration for certain. Once these celebrations, sponsored by the Washington leaders, had been regarded as "unofficial," and were so called. Now they had taken on a new dimension: the Inaugural Committee was regarded as official as the congressional committee responsible for the ceremonies at the Capitol. The celebration of the inauguration had taken on almost as official a role as had the oath-taking and the inaugural address.

For this inauguration, the House of Representatives laid claim to a share of the arrangements at the Capitol for President McKinley's swearing-in. For longer than anyone then could remember, this had been a prerogative of the Senate, but the House of Representatives would defer to the Senate in this no longer. For both inaugurations of George Washington, the House of Representatives and the Senate had appointed members to determine what arrangements would be appropriate, and again in 1805, for Jefferson's second inauguration, the House had shared in the proceedings. Thereafter, the Senate had made the arrangements for each President, not without some resentment from the House. In 1817, for example, Speaker of the House Henry Clay had refused to lend the House chamber to the Senate committee of arrangements for James Monroe's inauguration, because the Senators had insisted on bringing their own fine red chairs into the hall of the House for the ceremony. Clay told them that "the plain democratic chairs of the House were more becoming." As a result of this quarrel, Monroe was the first President to take the oath out-of-doors on the East Portico of the Capitol. In 1901, the ceremony had taken on more importance to the country and the world, and the House had its way. There would be joint committees of arrangements from then on. Significantly, Joseph G. Cannon of Illinois, one of the House's most powerful leaders, headed the House members on the 1901 committee of arrangements.

John Joy Edson, a prominent Washington banker and civic leader, was named Chairman of the Inaugural Committee. Assisting him was an executive committee of fifty-five members, many with long experience in these matters. Three of the members had been chairmen of previous Inaugural Committees, and some had been serving on Inaugural Committees since 1869 and 1873.

The finance committee raised a Guarantee Fund of more than $56,000, and came up with a new system to raise additional revenues. In recent inaugurations, the committee members had sold to outside interests various concessions and privileges. In 1901, for the first time, they erected their own reviewing stands for the inaugural parade and sold their own tickets. The committee only broke about even on the operation, but in inaugurations to follow, these tickets would help finance the celebration.

In another first, the 1901 Inaugural Committee appointed a committee on medals and badges to take the place of the committee on badges. This new body had the responsibility to procure the appropriate identity badges and to provide, for the first time, an inaugural medal for the Inaugural Committee's use. Chairman of the committee on medals and badges, General Ellis Spear, a prominent Washington patent attorney and businessman, received this directive: *This committee shall cause designs for medals and badges, and the cost thereof, to be submitted for the approval of the Inaugural Committee, and when so authorized it shall secure the same and deliver them to the chairmen of the several committees and officers for appropriate distribution.*

McKinley inaugural medal
Silver, 44 mm
Private collection

The decision had been made to strike inaugural medals as souvenirs for those who participated in putting on the celebrations. The badges would remain as the means of identifying committee members. The medals would be struck separately. This decision came naturally from the decision, in 1897, to strike a gold version of the inaugural badge for the President, and for the Vice President and inaugural chairman as well. What the Inaugural Committee had really decided this year was to designate the inaugural medal, which had evolved from the committee badges, as the official souvenir for the inauguration. The committee itself called it the "official medal" of the occasion. It would be struck in gold for the President, a fitting token for the chief of state of a world power.

Chairman Spear and his committee members tried to negotiate with the United States Mint at Philadelphia to make this inaugural medal, but the Mint would do no more than make the dies. The medals were struck by the Joseph K. Davison Company of Philadelphia, the same firm that had made the 1897 inaugural badge.

The committee did not report how many medals were struck and distributed to members. In all, the expenses ran to $1749.89, which suggests that the company struck about four thousand medals in bronze. Four years later, the same firm struck three thousand medals of the same size in bronze for the 1905 Inaugural Committee

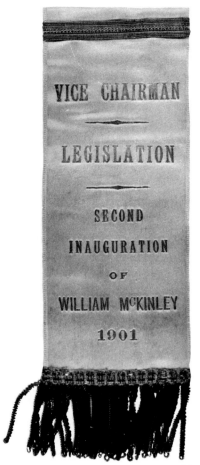

Legislative committee inaugural badge
Private collection

at a price of $1,000. Presumably, the 1901 committee also ordered gold medals for the Vice President and for Inaugural Chairman Edson, as well as one for President McKinley.

For the first time, the committee ordered some medals in silver. Housed in handsome presentation cases, these were given to the fifty-five members and officers of the inaugural executive committee. Some of its members chaired other committees, and in these instances, the presentation cases cited that chairmanship. Giving these silver medals to those most responsible for the success of the inauguration celebration was intended, obviously, as a special deference to them, in much the same way that the previous two Inaugural Committees had treated their executive committee members in silver-plating the medals on their badges.

The Davison Company had no sense that the designs or the dies for this medal of President McKinley belonged to the Inaugural Committee. A year and a half later, the company made badges for the thirty-sixth encampment of the Grand Army of the Republic, held in Washington. They used the reverse of the McKinley medal, with a different inscription, as the reverse of the G.A.R. medal.

WMcK	1901	1	gold	(44 mm)	presumably 3
WMcK	1901	2	silver	(44 mm)	55
WMcK	1901	3	bronze	(44 mm)	about 4,000

THEODORE
ROOSEVELT
1905

Under the rules adopted by the Inaugural Committee to govern the inauguration of Theodore Roosevelt on March 4, 1905, the committee on medals and badges was charged to "cause" the designing and production of inauguration medals "in the necessary quantity." This it proceeded to do, with General Ellis Spear again acting as chairman, as he had in 1901. Spear and his committee colleagues were not inclined to attempt more than was done for President McKinley four years before. They negotiated a contract with the same Philadelphia firm that had made the McKinley medals in 1901, a company now renamed Joseph K. Davison's Sons. For $1,000, the company agreed to provide 3,000 bronze medals by inauguration day. The firm also offered to strike the now customary gold medals for $55 each, and the silver medals for the members of the executive committee for $2.00 each. Brigadier General John M. Wilson, Chairman of the Inaugural Committee, approved the contract and signed it on January 28. The *Washington Post,* reporting on the arrangement, explained its purpose: "Every man who serves upon any of the subcommittees in charge of preparations for the inaugural ceremonies will receive an appropriate bronze medal as a token of the honor."

Neither the medals committee nor the private company made any effort at originality in designing President Roosevelt's inaugural medal. What they agreed to produce was simply a copy, in smaller size, of an existing medal. When Roosevelt had first become President in 1901, on the death of McKinley, the United States Mint struck the usual medal with his portrait, as the latest in its series of presidential

Roosevelt inaugural medal
Bronze, 44 mm
Private collection

medals. The portrait had been designed by Charles E. Barber (1840–1917), the Mint's chief engraver. Sculpting Roosevelt in left profile, Barber showed a somewhat somber man of forty-three. The reverse, modelled by Barber's assistant, George T. Morgan, was a design of a spray of oak and olive leaves coupled with the date on

Roosevelt 1901 Mint medal
Charles E. Barber and George T. Morgan
Bronze, 76 mm
Darrell C. Crain

which Roosevelt had first taken the oath: September 14, 1901. The Davison copyists in 1905 basically repeated the 1901 Mint medal, changing the inauguration date to March 4, 1905, and reducing its size. To complete the plagiarism, they eliminated the names of Barber and Morgan and substituted the Davison name on the reverse. By the testimony of this Davison medal, President Roosevelt looked in 1905 just the same way he did in 1901.

This medal did not please President Roosevelt. A man with interests and enthusiasms of astonishing variety, he had pronounced ideas on artistic matters, and he pursued them with the intensity that characterized so much of his life. Early in his presidency, he had drawn to his side American artists of outstanding abilities, and they became an informal cabinet of art advisers. With one of these, Frank Millet, Roosevelt discussed the Davison medal. Millet, a painter, spoke bluntly: the President's inaugural medal should come from the hands of a great artist, not a commercial journeyman. Millet suggested Augustus Saint-Gaudens, the greatest of living American sculptors.

Roosevelt, of course, knew Saint-Gaudens. They had been in correspondence for several years, and they had dined together. The President admired the sculptor's work with unrestrained zeal. In 1903, Roosevelt had written a letter in which he praised Saint-Gaudens's work so handsomely that the sculptor resolved to preserve it as a special treasure "so that when we have left the scene, my children's children may read it." Saint-Gaudens and Roosevelt had discussed in some detail the idea of altering and beautifying American coinage, and the sculptor had described to Roosevelt the high-relief coins of ancient Greece with a zest that Roosevelt caught and nourished. Even before Millet suggested Saint-Gaudens as the designer of Roosevelt's inaugural medal, the President had resolved to ask him to redesign the country's coinage.

Just when the inaugural medals committee was completing its negotiations with the Davison company, Saint-Gaudens had come to Washington on another matter. He visited the White House on January 18, 1905, and there President Roosevelt's Secretary of the Treasury, Leslie M. Shaw, asked the sculptor what he would charge to make new designs for American coins. The artist, then at the height of his powers and reputation, hesitated to commit himself to any such commission. It would be months before he finally agreed, for a fee of $5,000, to take the assignment. On the same day, January 18, Saint-Gaudens also met with the President, at which time Roosevelt asked him to make his inaugural medal.

Saint-Gaudens could not spare the time from his own crowded schedule to take on this new chore. Yet this was a personal request from the President; he could not totally reject it. Saint-Gaudens met with General Wilson, the Inaugural Committee chairman, and Wilson showed him the design that the committee had negotiated with the Davison company. That had to intensify Saint-Gauden's reluctance to turn down Roosevelt's request, for Charles Barber, who had modelled the Roosevelt portrait on the Davison medal, was an old foe. Saint-Gaudens as well had no admiration for the Davison company. "The man there who has charge of the bulk of ordinary medals already contracted for cannot possibly do artistic work," he told Roosevelt. "He is a commercial medalist with neither the means nor the power to rise above such an average."

Obviously, Saint-Gaudens did not feel he could abandon the President to this mediocrity. On the train back to New York City, he sketched designs for the obverse and the reverse of an inaugural medal. He knew what he wanted to achieve. Years before, he had studied carefully the medals of the Renaissance, notably those of the greatest of the medalists, Pisanello. Saint-Gaudens then had despaired of achieving such mastery himself. In time, however, he had won an international reputation for his portrait reliefs, and his early medals revealed his Renaissance tutoring. The one he designed in 1889 for the New York celebration of the one-hundredth anniversary of George Washington's first inauguration reflected Pisanello and the Renaissance in its balance, style, and lettering. Significantly, Saint-Gaudens had even had that medal cast in the Renaissance manner, and not struck. Designing a medal for the President, on so auspicious an occasion as his inauguration, Saint-Gaudens again drew from the inspiration of his Renaissance teachers.

Once back in New York City, Saint-Gaudens quickly contacted his one-time protégé, Adolph Weinman (1870–1952), then thirty-four years old, already fully into a great career as a sculptor himself. Weinman grasped at the chance to execute the models for the inaugural medal. Saint-Gaudens suggested a fee of $250, and Weinman immediately accepted. Saint-Gaudens then went to his club in New York, The Players, and wrote to the President. He had the project well in hand, and he wanted Roosevelt to know it. It was January 20.

The day before, even as Saint-Gaudens was sketching his ideas for the medal on the train back to New York City, President Roosevelt had asked General Wilson to make the formal request to the sculptor. Wilson sent a telegram to him that day and wrote him a longer letter. He explained that it was now customary to present gold medals to the President and Vice President on their inaugurations, and silver medals to the ranking members of the Inaugural Committee. Wilson was caught in an awkward position, because of the negotiations with the Davison company, but he resolved it by assigning the regular bronze medals to Davison and the gold and silver ones to Saint-Gaudens and another firm. Wilson told Saint-Gaudens that his medal should be one-and-three-quarters inches in diameter, the same size as the Davison medal.

"If the inauguration medal is to be ready for March the first," Saint-Gaudens wrote to Roosevelt, "there is not a moment to lose. I cannot do it, but I have arranged with the man best fitted to execute it in the country." He told the President about

Weinman, whose work he was certain Roosevelt would admire. "He has a most artistic nature, extremely diffident," Saint-Gaudens wrote. "He would do an admirable thing. He is also supple and takes suggestion intelligently."

The two artists had no difficulty working together. Saint-Gaudens was fifty-seven, a generation older than Weinman, and his former teacher. Weinman accepted Saint-Gaudens's designs with enthusiasm, obviously honored to collaborate with so great an artist on so significant a project.

Alarmed at the prospect that the Davison company might be given the contract to produce his medal, Saint-Gaudens sent Weinman to Philadelphia to talk to the firm's officials. He also had him write to General Wilson, to explain that Davison could not adequately reproduce the Saint-Gaudens–Weinman inaugural medal, and that it would have to be put into more artistic hands. Then Saint-Gaudens tried to enlist Roosevelt's help. "This is to beg you," he wrote to him, "to insist that the work be entrusted to Messrs. Tiffany or Gorham. Otherwise I would not answer for its being botched."

Weinman went to both New York firms and got from each its prices to make Saint-Gaudens's medals in gold, silver, and bronze. Gorham's figures were far higher than Tiffany's, and even Tiffany's deeply troubled General Wilson. He wrote to President Roosevelt about his fear that he and the committee would be "subjected to somewhat vicious attacks" if they agreed to pay Tiffany's prices, but he agreed to bear that burden if the President really wanted it so. "Every effort in my power will be made to comply with your wishes and those of Mr. Saint-Gaudens in regard to the inaugural medal," he wrote, "and they shall be carried out."

Saint-Gaudens, predictably, insisted that the medal he designed be far larger than the one-and-three-quarters inches that Wilson had requested. At one point, the sculptor believed the medal should be three-and-a-quarter inches in diameter, and only later decided to make it exactly three inches. That, too, increased costs. Saint-Gaudens also considered having the medals struck, in the normal manner, but later decided that they should be cast, in the Renaissance manner. That again raised costs, and moreover raised a whole new problem, because Tiffany's officers reported that there was difficulty in casting medals in silver, which would perhaps add additional costs. Briefly, Saint-Gaudens considered having the gold medals cast and the silver medals struck. The Inaugural Committee wanted a hundred medals in silver.

The Inaugural Committee met on the question on February 23, and decided to authorize two of the Saint-Gaudens medals in gold and 120 in bronze, all to be cast as desired. Wilson wrote to him: *The committee decided that it would deem it a sufficient honor for each of its members to have one of your superb medals in bronze, and therefore would require no silver medals. The committee thanks you most heartily for your courtesy and realizing that bronze can be cast much better than silver, prefers the bronze and will require no silver medals at all.*

Meanwhile, Saint-Gaudens had been perfecting his designs. In an early letter to the President, he described in some detail what he had so far done. "You know," he told Roosevelt, "the disposition of the design is nine-tenths of the battle." The sculptor's scheme was simplicity itself—the portrait on the obverse with only the President's name and title, and on the reverse a heroic eagle perched on a crag, with the inscription limited to the place and date of the inauguration. He had drawn again from the form and style of the Renaissance medalists. "The simplicity of the inscription aids the dignity of the arrangement," he explained to the President, "but if you believe that more is needed, I will add it with pleasure."

Columbian medal galvano (reverse)
Augustus Saint-Gaudens
Bronze, 203 mm
Saint-Gaudens National Historic Site

$10 gold piece (reverse) designed by
Augustus Saint-Gaudens in 1907, 25 mm
Private collection

On February 1, Saint-Gaudens wrote to Roosevelt's secretary, William Loeb, Jr., asking whether the President had a personal motto he would like used, or whether he would like the medal to include his campaign slogan "A Square Deal for Every Man." Loeb reported back that Roosevelt had no motto and thought the slogan "too colloquial" for use on a medal. Saint-Gaudens was not satisfied, and on February 10 he wrote to Loeb, asking whether the President would object to using "Aequum cuique" on the medal. Loeb checked with Roosevelt and then replied to Saint-Gaudens: "The President thinks 'Aequum cuique' first class and an excellent rendering of 'a square deal.'" (Translated literally, the Latin expression means "To each what is equitable.") With Roosevelt's permission, Saint-Gaudens added the Latin to the obverse of the medal.

The eagle Saint-Gaudens placed on the reverse of this medal was of special interest. The design was not new. Years before, in 1892, he had accepted a com-

59

*Plaster model (obverse) taken from the die of the Roosevelt inaugural medal
by Augustus Saint-Gaudens and Adolph Weinman, 77 mm (larger than the inaugural medal
because of the normal shrinkage which occurs in casting)*

mission from the United States Treasury to model the award medals for the World's
Columbian Exhibition at Chicago. John G. Carlisle, the Secretary of the Treasury,
readily enough accepted Saint-Gaudens's design for the obverse of the medal, a scene
of Columbus coming ashore in America, but he rejected out of hand three successive
models Saint-Gaudens had made for the reverse. On each of these, the artist had
included an eagle similar to the one he now used on President Roosevelt's inaugural
medal.

Saint-Gaudens, a diffident man in public matters, was nonetheless enraged at
this cavalier rejection by Treasury Secretary Carlisle, but there was a worse offense
to come. The Treasury commissioned another reverse for the Columbian medal, this
by Charles E. Barber, the Mint's own engraver and the very fellow whose portrait of
Theodore Roosevelt the Davison company was using on the 1905 inaugural medal.
Barber's model for the Columbian medal's reverse, a conventional design, clashed
unpleasantly with the obverse made by Saint-Gaudens. Angered, Saint-Gaudens
protested publicly this combining of Barber's work with his own, calling it an act of
"rare shamelessness." Now, in 1905, he had the opportunity to match his crafts-
manship against that of Barber on his inaugural medal for Theodore Roosevelt. Saint-
Gaudens had added cause to do his best. His use of the eagle from the rejected
reverses of 1892 suggests that he had not forgotten, nor forgiven, the rebuff he had
then received.

Saint-Gaudens especially liked this eagle. In 1907, he used it again, at President Roosevelt's request, for the reverse of the $10 gold piece he designed for the
government.

Whatever hopes Saint-Gaudens had to produce these medals by March 4,
inauguration day, were quickly abandoned. A stickler for detail, he oversaw every bit
of Weinman's work and then every stage of producing the medals themselves. Weinman worked his design on models ten inches in diameter. These had to be reduced,
and the new Janvier machine was used, but before that could be done, Weinman's
plaster models had to be cast in bronze. Then, after the models were reduced, plaster
casts were made of the medal in the new size for Saint-Gaudens's inspection.
Repeatedly the sculptor insisted that the work be done anew to higher perfection.
Tiffany & Company wanted its name placed on the medal, but Saint-Gaudens per-

mitted this only after the firm proved how inconspicuously it could be added to the rim. Saint-Gaudens would not allow the firm to send the gold medals to President Roosevelt and Vice President Charles Fairbanks until he had inspected them. By then it was late June, more than three months after the inauguration.

President Roosevelt approved the models as finished by Weinman. Years later, Weinman told his son Robert, himself a sculptor, what had happened. He had taken the models to Washington for Roosevelt's approval, and they were set up in a room at the White House to await the President's inspection. "Teddy Roosevelt came in about 80 miles an hour," Robert reported, "said 'Bully, bully' and dashed out."

Besides the gold medal, the Inaugural Committee gave Roosevelt thirty-five replicas in bronze, for him to distribute. Committee members received eighty-two of the bronze replicas, and three were given to prominent libraries. That meant there were none of the 120 left for Saint-Gaudens. He wrote to General Wilson about this, and the inaugural chairman authorized Tiffany to cast the five that Saint-Gaudens wanted. Wilson wrote to Saint-Gaudens that the committee deliberately was resisting pressures to make more of the medals because the members did not want it to become "too common as has been the case in previous inaugurations." Later, Wilson himself received a copy of the Saint-Gaudens medal in gold. He donated it to the United States Government, and it is now housed in the Smithsonian Institution.

Despite a broken die that delayed production for ten days, the three thousand Davison medals were delivered on March 2, two days ahead of the inauguration. The company struck two varieties, some on thin planchets, the others on planchets almost twice as thick. "They were distributed as promptly as possible," the medals committee reported, "and apparently were satisfactory to those who received them."

The members of the medals committee were aware of what had resulted from their original decision to have the Davison firm produce the inexpensive, conventional inaugural medals. Artistically they could not be compared to the medals produced by Saint-Gaudens and Weinman. The committee had nothing to do with the medals cast by Tiffany, other than to pay for their making. They knew, however, what Saint-Gaudens and Weinman had achieved. As their report stated, "they were superb works of art."

President Roosevelt had the same reaction when he finally received his gold inaugural medal along with the replicas in bronze. He was at his home in Oyster Bay, New York, for his summer holiday. He could scarcely contain his enthusiasm as he wrote a thank-you letter to the artist: "My dear fellow, I am very grateful to you, and I am very proud to have been able to associate you in some way with my administration. I like the medals *immensely;* but that goes without saying; for the work is eminently characteristic of you."

Reading the typed letter over before he signed it, he was not satisfied. "Thank Heaven," he scribbled into the text, "we have at last some artistic work of permanent worth done for the government."

Still not satisfied, Roosevelt added a postscript in his hand: "I don't want to slop over; but I feel just as if we had suddenly imported a little of Greece of the 5th or 4th centuries B.C into America; and am very proud and very grateful that I happen to be the beneficiary."

TR	1905	1	Tiffany	gold	(74 mm)	3
TR	1905	2	Tiffany	bronze	(74 mm)	125
TR	1905	3	Joseph K. Davison's Sons	bronze	(44 mm)	3,000

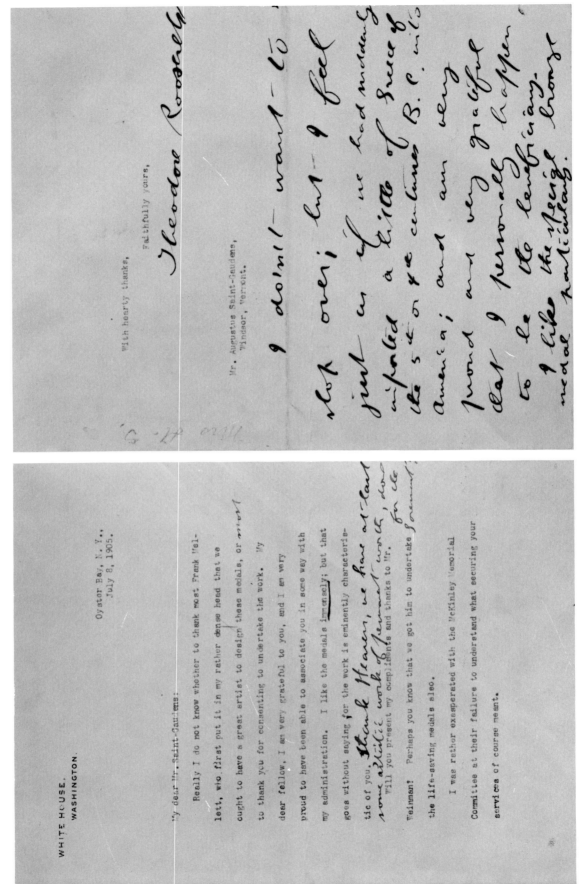

WHITE HOUSE.
WASHINGTON.

Oyster Bay, N. Y.,
July 8, 1905.

My dear Mr. Saint-Gaudens:

Really I do not know whether to thank most Frank Millett, who first put it in my rather dense head that we ought to have a great artist to design these medals, or *you* for consenting to undertake the work. My dear fellow, I am very grateful to you, and I am very proud to have been able to associate you in some way with my administration. I like the medals immensely; but that goes without saying for the work is eminently characteristic of you. Thank Heaven, we have at last some artistic work of permanent worth. Will you present my compliments and thanks to Mr. Weinman? Perhaps you know that we got him to undertake the life-saving medals also.

I was rather exasperated with the McKinley Memorial Committee at their failure to understand what securing your services of course meant.

With hearty thanks,

Faithfully yours,

Theodore Roosevelt

Mr. Augustus Saint-Gaudens,
Windsor, Vermont.

I don't want to [?] not over; but — I feel just as if we had managed to unfold a little of Greece of the 5th to 4th centuries B.C. into America; and am very proud and very grateful that I personally happen to be the beneficiary. I like the design bronze medal particularly.

Letter, Theodore Roosevelt to Augustus Saint-Gaudens, July 8, 1905
Dartmouth College Library

62

WILLIAM H. TAFT
1909

In 1908, as his second term as President approached its close, Theodore Roosevelt was only forty-nine. Unhappily for him, he had pledged that he would not seek another term and, reluctantly, he had to step aside. Roosevelt, however, still held full command of his party, and at his bidding the Republican National Convention nominated William Howard Taft for President, and James Schoolcraft Sherman for Vice President. They were overwhelmingly elected in November 1908. Frank H. Hitchcock designated Edward J. Stellwagon, a Washington banker, as Chairman of the Inaugural Committee. "By an established custom," Hitchcock told Stellwagon, "it falls to me as Chairman of the Republican National Committee to arrange for the organization of a citizens' committee to take charge of the ceremonies attending the inauguration of the President-elect." Stellwagon, as required, appointed the other officials, including Richard Norris Brooke as chairman of the medals and badges committee.

Brooke, an artist, was vice principal of the Corcoran school of art, and sometime president of the Society of Washington Artists. He had studied painting at the Pennsylvania Academy of Fine Arts and later in Paris. He deliberately appointed committee members who could give assurance that they would commission a worthy inaugural medal for President Taft. No less than five members, including Brooke, were artists in their own right. Three others were engaged in vocations that the committee itself described as "calling for the constant exercise of artistic taste." Four of those appointed brought experience from previous inaugural medals and badges committees. "It was sought," as the report stated, "to enroll a body favorable to the most satisfactory results."

Among the artists on this committee was painter Frank Millet, who had advised President Roosevelt to seek the great artist, Augustus Saint-Gaudens, to model his inaugural medal. Unfortunately, Millet could not recommend Saint-Gaudens again; he had died in 1907.

The medals committee did make an earnest, serious attempt to obtain a major artist to design the medal for President Taft. They chose Victor D. Brenner (1871–1924), a medalist of outstanding talent and reputation, to make the new inaugural medal. Brenner had been discovered and befriended by President Roosevelt. While modelling a portrait of Roosevelt, Brenner had shown him a model he had made for a plaquette of Abraham Lincoln. Roosevelt liked it so much that he arranged with the Treasury Department to use it as a new design for the penny. Choosing such a medalist, the committee felt assured of a sensitive, telling portrait of President Taft.

The members of the committee, of course, knew perfectly well the artistic triumph that Saint-Gaudens and Adolf Weinman had achieved in creating the inauguration medal for President Roosevelt in 1905. Doubtlessly, it was this that prompted them to commission the best medalist they could obtain for the job, and that medalist, Victor Brenner, assuredly also knew what Saint-Gaudens and Wein-

63

Inaugural parade held in the worst weather on record, March 4, 1909
Library of Congress

man had achieved. Brenner had to know as well that the Saint-Gaudens medal had not been quickly made. Originally, Saint-Gaudens had spoken of completing that medal by inauguration day, March 4, but, in reality, it had not been possible to produce it on time. In fact, Roosevelt did not receive his gold medal until fully four months after his inauguration.

That delay had been agreeable at the time. After all, it was the President himself who had asked for this special medal from this great artist. Moreover, the committee then had another medal, the one produced by the Davison company, on hand for distribution on inauguration day. The 1909 committee gave Victor Brenner no such time as Saint-Gaudens had been allowed.

Since memory served, the inaugural medals and badges had always been ready by inauguration day. That was their purpose. They were not just a memento; they were identification for those engaged in running the inauguration celebrations. The medals committee gave Brenner only until March 4 to have his medal ready, and Brenner discovered belatedly that "the allowance of time," in the committee's words, was "too short." On reconsideration, Brenner felt he had to turn down the commission.

Brenner, of course, was not the only sculptor or medalist available for the commission. Indeed, a school of talented medalists had emerged in these years, but the time constraint that had prevented Brenner from proceeding would have the same effect on any other member of this group. Reluctantly, and obviously unhappily, the committee turned to a commercial medal-maker.

Even so, the committee members tried to impose conditions on the private company to enhance the quality of this inaugural medal. They awarded the contract to Joseph K. Davison's Sons in Philadelphia, the same newly renamed firm that had

64

Roosevelt inaugural medal
Augustus Saint-Gaudens and Adolph Weinman
Gold, 74 mm
Division of Political History, Smithsonian Institution

UNION LEAGUE of MD.

WASHINGTON
MARCH 4,
1905

INAUGURATION

WASHINGTON, D. C.
MARCH 4, 1905
MINNEAPOLIS
REPUBLICAN
FLAMBEAU CLUB

KINGS COUNTY
Republican Organization

INAUGURATION
Theodore Roosevelt
WASHINGTON

MARCH 4TH, 1905

Union Co.   Republican Com.

INAUGURATION
OF
ROOSEVELT
AND
FAIRBANKS

WASHINGTON, D. C.
MARCH 4, 1905

WASHINGTON, D.C.
March 4th 1905

WASHINGTON, D.C.
March 4th 1905

WASHINGTON, D.C.
March 4th 1905

WASHINGTON, D.C.
March 4th 1905

PENNSYLVANIA

LEGISLATURE
INAUGURATION
Washington, D.C.
MARCH 4th,

INAUGURATION, 1905

ROOSEVELT
AND
FAIRBANKS

The
Republican
Club
OF THE CITY OF
New York

Theodore Roosevelt inaugural badges
Private collection

2d Lieutenant

PHELPS GUARDS
PATERSON, N. J.

ROOSEVELT AND FAIRBANKS

INAUGURATION

PETER E. SMITH

MARCHING
C·L·U·B
PHILADELPHIA

INAUGURATION
WASHINGTON
ROOSEVELT
FAIRBANKS 4TH

PHILADELPHIA

DAVID MARTIN
MARCHING CLUB
19TH WARD

INAUGURATION

WASHINGTON, D. C.

1905

Republican County Committee
County of New York

INAUGURATION

WASHINGTON, D. C.

MARCH 4, 1905

ST. PAUL, MINN.

WASHINGTON, D. C.
MARCH 4, 1905

Frelinghuysen Lancers

NEWARK, N. J.

INAUGURATION

MARCH 4, 1905

WASHINGTON, D. C.

Commercial
CLUB
Of Pittsburg

Inauguration
OF ROOSEVELT
1905

PENNSYLVANIA

LEGISLATURE
INAUGURATION
Washington, D.C.
MARCH 4TH

PUBLIC ORDER
POLICE
MARCH 4, 1905

INAUGURATION
MARCH 4TH

Medals, sold by street vendors, for various presidential inaugurations
Private collection

made inaugural medals in 1901 and 1905 and the inaugural badge in 1897. The committee asked the company "to furnish a medal larger in size, more artistic in style, and more elaborate in finish than the usual commercial medal." That language suggested not just what the committee wanted, but also what it expected to receive from a commercial firm.

The committee members, all the same, had a cautious eye on the price. The contract provided terms they regarded as "reasonable"—three thousand medals in bronze, for $1,400, and three medals in gold, for $250.

Apparently, they at first planned to continue the tradition of striking a special version for ranking officials of the Inaugural Committee. They indicated at one point their intention to strike fifty of the Taft inauguration medals in silver, and the *American Journal of Numismatics* reported that these silver medals would be given to members of President Taft's cabinet and "others prominent in political circles," presumably ranking officers of the Inaugural Committee. No medals were struck in silver, however, and the committee's report gave no explanation.

The Roosevelt inaugural medal of 1905 and the McKinley inaugural medal of 1901 used only the President's portrait. The 1909 committee decided to add the portrait of Vice President Sherman to the inaugural medal. In doing so, the committee returned to the practice of 1889, 1893, and 1897, when jugate portraits of the President and Vice President had been used on the medals for the inaugural badges.

There was no thought, apparently, of asking either Taft or Sherman to pose for the commercial medalist, but the committee members arranged for the next best thing. They hired private photographers to take a series of pictures of both Taft and Sherman. The Davison designer worked from these photographs.

The Taft–Sherman medal that Davison produced could not rival the Tiffany medal made four years earlier for President Roosevelt, but certainly it was a cut above the other medal the firm had made, in the same year, for Roosevelt. It carried original portraits of the President and Vice President, but more than that, it showed how a commercial firm could produce, for an occasion such as an inauguration, a better than conventional product.

Still, it must have disappointed the artists on the medals committee. The reverse merely carried the names and titles of the President and Vice President. They had hoped for something grander, more eloquent, but they had to know the

Taft–Sherman inaugural medal
Gold, 51 mm
Reverend Hector L. Bolduc

limits of the Davison firm. As Saint-Gaudens had said, its artisans had "neither the means nor the power" to create truly artistic work. The Taft medal proved attractive enough, however, to encourage its duplication in a cheap, cast imitation.

The inauguration itself proved a success, despite a blizzard so severe that President Taft had to take the oath of office in the Senate chamber. Happily, the Inaugural Committee sold tickets enough for the grandstands and to the ball to pay all expenses and repay the Guarantee Fund of $86,720 in full. The medals committee had been allotted $2,300 and had stayed within that limit by a little over $100.

Inaugural Committee members presented the gold medals to President Taft and Vice President Sherman without a formal ceremony. They also gave both men an especially handsomely printed, gold-mounted pamphlet, featuring a brief biography of Taft written for the occasion by President Roosevelt. This was designated the official souvenir of the inauguration. From the White House on March 8, President Taft wrote a thank-you note to Inauguration Chairman Stellwagon, who had received the third Taft inaugural medal struck in gold. Taft said he thought the gold medal was "beautiful." He liked the pamphlet too. "I am delighted," he wrote, "to have them as remembrances of the occasion."

| WHT | 1909 | 1 | gold | (51 mm) | 3 |
| WHT | 1909 | 2 | bronze | (51 mm) | 3,000 |

WOODROW
WILSON
1913

In 1912, President Taft sought reelection, but he was challenged by Theodore Roosevelt, who ran as an independent on the so-called "Bull Moose" ticket. The resulting split of the Republican vote gave the election to Woodrow Wilson, then the Governor of New Jersey. Elected Vice President was Thomas Riley Marshall, the Governor of Indiana.

Even though Wilson's election ushered in the first Democratic administration in twenty years, that did not unduly alter the traditional practices of the inaugural celebrations. Now the Democratic National Chairman, William F. McCombs, chose the Chairman of the Inaugural Committee. He picked William Corcoran Eustis, a Washingtonian of considerable local prominence, and Eustis, in turn, chose the chairmen of the operating committees. The traditions of these committees, however, ran far deeper than partisan politics. The citizens of Washington had long since taken the celebration of presidential inaugurations as their special responsibility, and many of them served in that function regardless of the President-elect's political party. It was so in 1913.

Eustis named the artist Richard Norris Brooke again as chairman of the medals and badges committee. Brooke named ten members to his committee, five of whom had served with him in 1909. An addition this year was Henry K. Bush-Brown (1857–1935), a local sculptor of talent who, sixteen years later, would model the inaugural medal for President Herbert Hoover. Plainly, this experienced committee meant to get the best medal possible under the limits of time and circumstance.

The medals committee members made no effort this time to persuade a sculptor of high reputation to take the commission for the Wilson inaugural medal. They did decide to change the manufacturer, giving the contract to Whitehead & Hoag of Newark, New Jersey. They negotiated for an artist skilled beyond the normal talents of mere commercialism. Brooke and his colleagues knew what they wanted. "Bearing in mind the growing impressiveness of Inaugural ceremonies, and their fugitive nature," he reported, "the Committee has sought to provide a medal fittingly commemorative of so august an event."

This committee attempted to achieve precisely what President Roosevelt had wanted back in 1905—a medal of artistic merit worthy of the occasion. They had also sought that in 1909, only to become aware of the imperatives imposed on them to deliver the medals by inauguration day. The time limit forced compromise, but this committee in 1913 knew in advance that compromise was mandatory and how to make the best of it.

Clearly, however, the presidential inaugural medal, as an entity, as a tradition, had begun to take on a life of its own. Only since 1889 had there been inaugural medals that could be considered "official" or "commissioned," and for half these commissions, those in charge had sought with considerable diligence to create a medal of high quality. In the larger sense, they were seeking to create a new art form.

The members of the 1913 committee believed that they had succeeded in what they had set out to do, even if their objective had not been as ambitious as that of President Roosevelt and Saint-Gaudens eight years before. "Though limitation of time forbade recourse for this work to some sculptor of international celebrity," Committee Chairman Brooke reported, in the stilted manner of committee chairmen, "the services of a well-trained professional artist, who was also an expert die-cutter, were secured by the manufacturers for the production of the Inaugural Medal, the result being a medal which, for size, execution and dignity of design, measurably meets the requirements of the occasion."

Wilson "sample" inaugural medal
Bronze, 7C mm
Private collection

The committee members did not merely turn the contract over to Whitehead & Hoag and hope for the best. Clearly, they did not give the company a free hand to produce a medal of its own choosing. Chairman Brooke, for example, went to Newark to check the progress of the medals at the factory. There are extant replicas of the Wilson inaugural medal which clearly indicate that the committee members approved the medal before authorizing full production. These bronze replicas do not carry the firm's imprint on their rims, as do the finished medals, and they are stamped "sample" on obverse and reverse. The company appears, therefore, to have made some advance copies for the committee's consideration. As such, they are a variety separate from the regular issue.

Once the committee members had approved the medal, they authorized the company to strike three thousand in bronze, thirty in silver, and three in gold. The gold medals, as now traditionally, went to the President, the Vice President, and the Chairman of the Inaugural Committee. The silver medals went to the chairmen of the lesser committees and the ranking officers of the Inaugural Committee. The bronze medals, as usual, were given to all the others who had helped.

The medals committee members felt pleased with their handiwork, so pleased that they considered ordering an additional eight hundred. The chairman's report spoke of the committee's sense of indebtedness to the company which had "in many particulars exceeded the terms of the contract." They had a right to feel pleased.

The unnamed artist had designed a medal of classical simplicity. He had as well drawn a sensitive portrait of the new President. Woodrow Wilson normally wore eyeglasses, but at the request of the medals committee the artist omitted them in this portrait. Larger than the three previous inaugural medals made by the Davison company, this one was enhanced by its size. The Taft medal had been made two inches in diameter. The Wilson medal measured two-and-three-quarters inches in diameter, a dramatic difference. In time, the two-and-three-quarters-inch size would become standard.

The Whitehead & Hoag Company had no sense that the design of this medal

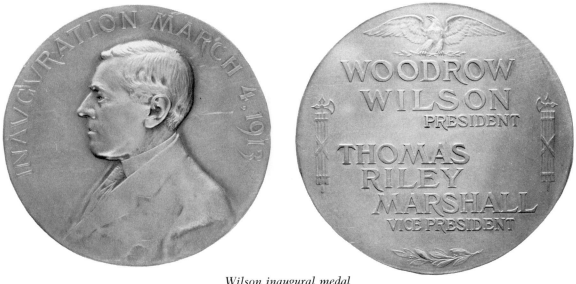

Wilson inaugural medal
Gold, 70 mm
Woodrow Wilson House

belonged to the Inaugural Committee. The firm felt free to use the portrait of Wilson on other medals, and did. This was not new, for as we have seen, the firm of Joseph K. Davison's Sons had used the reverse of the 1901 McKinley inaugural medal afterwards on at least one other medal. In 1913, Whitehead & Hoag made a special inaugural badge for the Indiana Democratic Club, whose members obviously were proud that native-son Thomas Riley Marshall had been elected Vice President. The Indianians provided Marshall with a guard of honor for the inauguration. For the members of the Indiana Democratic Club, Whitehead & Hoag made a badge with a variation of the same Wilson portrait on the obverse of the medal and a striking portrait of Marshall on the reverse. The similarity of style suggests that both portraits came from the same artist.

A year later, Whitehead & Hoag used the same Wilson portrait for still another medal, this one struck to commemorate the establishment of the Federal Reserve banks, a major accomplishment of the Wilson administration. The medal's reverse was blank.

The Inaugural Committee, as usual, had planned all the now traditional celebrations of the new President's inauguration: the parade, the fireworks, and the ball, as well as the medal. In the midst of the preparations, word came unexpectedly from President-elect Wilson that there would be no inaugural ball. Wilson offered no explanation of this decision. The news shocked Washington, especially those who

*Wilson–Marshall inaugural badge made
for the Indiana Democratic Club
Bronze, 51 mm
Private collection*

had long been involved with running the inaugurations. Not until some years later was the reason for the cancellation fully known. Josephus Daniels, an intimate of the President-elect and soon to be the Secretary of the Navy in his cabinet, had traveled to New Jersey to consult with him. There, Daniels met Mrs. Wilson, who was the daughter and granddaughter of Presbyterian ministers. "What do you think of the propriety of an inaugural ball when Woodrow is inaugurated?" she asked him.

Daniels explained that inaugural balls were of long-standing tradition, that they were somewhat "commercialized," in that anyone with the price of a ticket could attend, and that social Washington as well as the shopkeepers who sold dresses would raise a storm if the ball were cancelled.

"I cannot bear to think of Woodrow's inauguration being attended with a ball in which all sorts of people would engage in these modern dances, which I do not like," Mrs. Wilson said. A religious woman, Mrs. Wilson gave Daniels her view that her husband's inauguration was a quasi-religious ceremony, a solemn consecration of her husband to a sacred mission. She viewed the ball as a desecration. It was she who had vetoed it.

There were protests, including some from the Inaugural Committee, but Mrs. Wilson, acting through her husband, was adamant. More was involved, of course, than the social aspects of the ball or the losses to the shopkeepers. For many years, the sale of tickets to the balls had provided the principal means for each Inaugural Committee to finance its operations. The balls had helped pay for the fireworks, the hospitality to visitors, the special decorations for the city, and the medals.

Federal Reserve Bank medal, 1914,
on which the inaugural portrait of 1913 was used
Bronze, 70 mm
Private collection

Mrs. Wilson's cancellation of the ball cost the 1913 Inaugural Committee dearly. As a result, the committee actually spent more than its receipts. For the first time, the subscribers to the Guarantee Fund were not repaid in full. Usually, each Inaugural Committee turned enough profit not only to repay the Guarantee Fund but also to make a donation to local charities. This year, the committee suffered a loss of more than $5,000. The medals that were given away cost $2,030, a substantial part of that loss. It was an ominous sign for the continuation of the inaugural medal tradition, for it would be twenty years before another Inaugural Committee again ran an official ball. In that time, the tradition of the inaugural medal barely survived, and finally only because their making and distribution were placed on a different financial basis.

The Inaugural Committee, with due solemnity, presented gold medals to both President Wilson and Vice President Marshall. Each seemed to like the medal he received. "As a work of art," Marshall wrote to the committee in thanks, "it could hardly be surpassed." President Wilson also sent his "cordial" thanks. "I am indeed glad to have it," he wrote, "and I prize it all the more highly because it is a memento of an occasion and a ceremony whose every detail of arrangements was admirably planned and flawlessly executed. . . ."

WW	1913	1	gold	(70 mm)	3
WW	1913	2	silver	(70 mm)	30
WW	1913	3	bronze	(70 mm)	3,000
WW	1913	4	bronze	(70 mm) marked "sample"	unknown, probably less than 12

WOODROW
WILSON
1917

Woodrow Wilson campaigned successfully for reelection as President on the slogan "He kept us out of war." The conflict had raged through Europe since the summer of 1914, and in the months after the 1916 presidential election, the United States moved steadily toward participation in that war, despite President Wilson's efforts to the contrary. On January 31, the German ambassador delivered a note informing the American government that Germany would unleash unlimited submarine warfare on all sea traffic. In February, Wilson learned that Germany had secretly proposed, in the event of war with the United States, an alliance with Mexico whereby Mexico would attack the United States to reconquer her lost territories in Texas, New Mexico, and Arizona. Obviously, under such circumstances, a gala celebration of Wilson's second inauguration would hardly have seemed appropriate.

In mid-December, President Wilson had hopes of leading the warring countries to peace: on December 18 he sent identical notes to all the belligerent countries proposing an end to the war on mutually acceptable terms and a "guarantee" against future wars. On December 11, a little over a month after the election, the Democratic National Chairman, Vance McCormick, appointed Colonel Robert N. Harper, a Washington banker, as Chairman of the Inaugural Committee. There were no reasons then for Colonel Harper not to plan a full-scale inauguration celebration, including a ball. The President's wife, Ellen Axson Wilson, who had prevented the ball in 1913, had died in August 1914. In December 1915, he had married Edith Bolling Galt, a vivacious and charming widow, who scarcely would have opposed a ball on religious-moral grounds. In preparation for a full celebration, the Inaugural Committee collected a Guarantee Fund of $68,000, the largest fund prior to President Taft's inauguration.

Chairman Harper had appointed a committee on medals and badges, with D. S. Callahan, a Washington businessman, as chairman. Callahan promptly called the group into session and began to arrange for the usual three gold inaugural medals and the usual three thousand replicas in bronze. The committee had not proceeded far when its members were notified that they would have to cut expenditures whereever possible.

Because of the gravity of the international situation, the ball had been cancelled. That meant serious financial difficulties, for, as in previous inaugurations, the Inaugural Committee counted on the sale of tickets to the ball largely to finance the other activities. Arthur Peter, chairman of the finance committee, looked back at the grim prospects in his report: "The war, the absence of the inaugural ball, and the doubt which for some time existed whether there would be an inaugural ceremony made it apparent that there would be a deficit." The danger of international hostilities was not exaggerated: just four weeks after the inaugural ceremony, President Wilson asked Congress to declare war on Germany and her allied powers.

The medals committee met and unanimously recommended that this year the Inaugural Committee not give out bronze replicas to those working on the inauguration activities. That would be a saving. However, they did recommend that the traditional gold medal be struck for the President, the Vice President, and the Chairman of the Inaugural Committee, and they obtained permission for this. Inaugural Chairman Harper, however, asked the medals committee not to make a gold medal for him because of the financial restraints.

Under the rules governing the various committees, the medals committee this year was instructed "as far as possible" to let all contracts with local Washington firms. This was an innovation, perhaps instigated by pressures from the local merchants. In any event, it effectively prevented the medals committee from approaching the Whitehead & Hoag Company, or any other out-of-town company. Thus it was that the medals committee gave the contract to R. Harris & Company, a Washington firm whose principal business was making and selling jewelry and trophies, and occasionally medals. The parochialism of this rule ran totally contrary to the efforts by three preceding medals committees to create, in the President's medals, a genuine work of art. These committees sought, as best they could, a sculptor of repute to design the medal, and in this area they had no restrictions. Although these previous medals committees were dominated by artists and those sympathetic to artistic achievement, the chairman of the 1917 committee, D. J. Callahan, was president of the Rotary Club of Washington, D.C., a position hardly suited for resisting the pressures of local businessmen.

The firm that received the contract to make three gold inaugural medals for a fee of $425, had on its staff a thirty-seven-year-old engraver, Darrell C. Crain, and it was he who designed the medal for President Wilson's second inauguration. Crain was primarily an engraver and designer of jewelry, not a medalist.

For obvious reasons of cost, the committee ordered a medal smaller than the one in 1913. The 1917 medals, the same size as the Taft inaugural medal of 1909, measured two inches. For reasons unknown, the engraver made the President's portrait so tiny as to render it difficult to identify. Wilson, although the central figure, is flanked by two women, and appears as part of a larger design. He seems grave and somber, as befitting the times. For the reverse, engraver Crain merely designed a variation of the reverse of the 1913 medal.

The designer used the traditional date, March 4, as the inauguration date in 1917, although the actual public ceremony took place on March 5. That year March 4

Wilson inaugural medal
Darrell C. Crain
Gold, 51 mm
Woodrow Wilson House

fell on a Sunday. Therefore Wilson took the oath privately at the White House that day and publicly on the Capitol steps the next day.

The medals committee members were pleased enough with Crain's designs: "These gold medals . . . are beautiful, both in design and character, and the work of the artist well merited our recommendation."

Of course, they did not authorize any bronze medals, those usually distributed to committee members. The manufacturer made some nevertheless. How many bronze medals were struck is not known; the company's records long since have been discarded. The scarcity of these medals, however, suggests that the number was not more than two or three hundred. The medal used as illustration in the Inaugural Committee's formal report has been identified as a bronze. It may have been a trial strike made for the committee's approval. Doubtlessly, the Inaugural Committee members and others purchased bronze medals from this local firm. Not many of these medals were struck because the obverse die cracked. The crack, beneath Wilson's portrait, stretched from the final "s" in "Preparedness" to the right foot of the female figure to the right of Wilson's portrait. The bronze medals came in two clearly separate varieties. One was fully finished with the firm's name stamped on the rim, and the other lacks the rim marking and the finish. This suggests that the company put a patina only on the medals sold, and that more were struck than sold.

If the committee could not provide bronze medals, it could and did provide a memento. This was a specially designed badge with a bronze pin bearing the designation "Inaugural Committee," and a metal bar hanger with the member's name. The committee had 226 of these made, and presented them to members of the Inaugural Committee and all chairmen and vice chairmen of subordinate committees. These were in addition to the 3,495 regular badges ordered.

The Harris company struck at least one of the Wilson inaugural medals in silver. The artist received this medal, and he engraved his own last name, "Crain," on its rim in place of that of the firm. Despite Chairman Harper's request not to strike a gold medal for him, the medals committee did so anyway. Medals Committee Chairman Callahan presented it to Harper, as a surprise, at a final meeting of the Inaugural Committee on March 28, 1917. Callahan told Harper that they had decided that he should have the gold medal as a souvenir, despite his protest, not for its intrinsic value alone, but to commemorate his services.

The dire financial forecasts for this inauguration proved well founded. The medals and badges committee stayed within its allotment, but most of the other committees were unable to do so, and overspent by more than $10,000 in all. With the normally substantial revenues from an inaugural ball lost, the committee had to depend primarily on the sale of tickets to the reviewing stands for the inaugural parade. These sales proved so disappointing, however, that the Inaugural Committee did not recoup even the money it had spent to build the stands. Overall, the Inaugural Committee lost more than $23,000 on its various activities, and therefore could repay the contributors to the Guarantee Fund only two-thirds of what they had advanced. Thus, this was the second consecutive inauguration celebration operated at a financial loss. That jeopardized anew the future of presidential inaugural medals.

This year, for the first time, the Inaugural Committee had felt it necessary to cancel the practice of giving replicas in bronze of the President's inaugural medal to those who helped inaugurate him. It just could not afford the expense. That consideration of cost seemed at this point about to doom the graceful tradition, now almost well established, of a formal presidential inaugural medal.

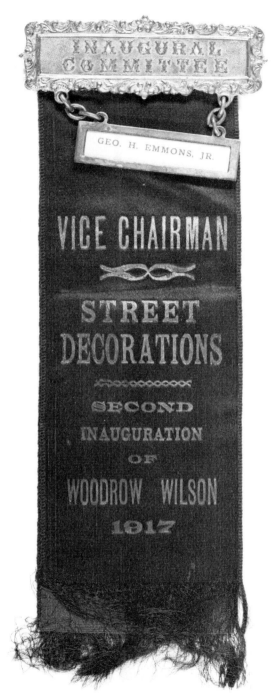

Street decorations committee inaugural badge
Private collection

WW	1917	1	gold	(51 mm)	3
WW	1917	2	silver	(51 mm)	1 known
WW	1917	3	bronze	(51 mm)	unknown, probably not more than 300

WARREN G. HARDING
1921

Warren G. Harding won an overwhelming victory in the 1920 presidential election, and his victory signalled more than a Republican triumph over the Democratic candidate, Governor James S. Cox of Ohio, whose running mate was Franklin D. Roosevelt. At stake for the Democrats was also the plan President Woodrow Wilson had devised to bring the United States more actively into world affairs. For the Republicans, however, the election of Harding meant a repudiation of Wilsonianism, not just his internationalism, but his prim personal deportment. The inauguration of Harding would restore gaiety to the national capital. President-elect Harding chose his friend Edward "Ned" McLean, playboy publisher of the *Washington Post*, as chairman of his Inaugural Committee.

McLean was a man of great wealth, married to the daughter of Thomas F. Walsh, who had made a fortune in Colorado mining. The McLeans owned an enormous house in Washington, where they were known for their extravagant party-giving. Evalyn McLean, as one of her baubles, owned the fabled Hope Diamond.

Harding knew what kind of an inauguration he wanted, and he had so signalled McLean. From Marion, Ohio, Harding's home town, came word that this would be "the most dazzling celebration in the memory of the present generation." A Washington newspaper hailed the coming return of the inaugural ball "in a blaze of glory" after "an exile" of eight years. What Ned McLean wanted was described by his wife in *Father Struck it Rich*, her autobiography: *What he wished to have was an affair about ten times as lively as a Fourth of July celebration combined with the ending of a victorious war. There were to have been fireworks displays, bands by the score, and all manner of excitement to mark the passage of executive power from Wilson's hands to those of Harding.* What was planned was a return to the inaugural celebrations of years gone by—a parade, a ball, a concert, a dazzling fireworks display and, of course, medals for the President, the Vice President, and all those who helped make this inauguration the celebration McLean hoped it would be. The tradition of inaugural medals had barely survived Woodrow Wilson's presidency and the advent of World War I. Now, again, the medal seemed assured of restoration.

Chairman McLean's plans were not to be. In the 1920 election campaign, Republican orators had denounced the extravagances of Wilson's Democratic administration, and they had done this effectively with the voters. Not only did their campaign oratory help create a national anti-extravagance attitude, but the Republicans had left themselves open to countercharges, from the congressional Democrats, against the kind of inauguration McLean was planning for Harding. What was equally a matter of political sensitivity, the national economy had turned sour and a depression was at hand. By January 1921, there were one million American workers unemployed, and there were forecasts that by March those without jobs would number four million. "Then," wrote Mrs. McLean in her autobiography, "Senator Borah and some others began to squawk about the cost of all this to the government."

76

William Borah of Idaho, indeed, took the Senate floor to denounce all these plans for a gala inaugural celebration. He cited the government costs involved: $50,000 to build the inaugural stand at the Capitol, $60,000 for extra police, $37,000 to transport the West Point cadets to Washington, $25,000 to bring the Naval Academy's midshipmen, and $200,000 to fix the Pension Building for the inaugural ball. "Mr. President," Borah said, sarcastically, "that is a good beginning for an administration which is pledged, or you might say, consecrated, to economy." He argued that Harding's inauguration would cost the federal government $1 million at a time when the national budget showed a deficit of $1 billion. He had touched a sensitive spot. Soon the Senate was engaged in a full-scale debate on Harding's extravagance. *It seems to me,* said Senator Duncan Fletcher of Florida, *that now, when the whole world is staggering under debt, and there is suffering and distress everywhere, when our people are complaining about taxes, and properly so, many of them unescapable as the necessary consequences of a world upheaval and the greatest war in all history, we ought to endeavor to hold down these expenditures out of the public Treasury to the very limit. This is no time . . . to indulge in these extravagant parades and demonstrations and celebrations.*

Someone who signed himself the chairman of the Harding and Coolidge Republican League sent Harding a telegram of great length, protesting McLean's inauguration celebration plans. At this point, Harding did not want to abandon them. In an account by Mrs. McLean, the President-elect "had Harry Daugherty try to straighten out the mess. His instructions were to 'see this party and pour oil on troubled waters if possible.'" Daugherty, soon to be Harding's attorney general, could not resolve the matter that easily. The Senate debate had taken place on January 4 and 5. On January 10, a similar debate broke out in the House of Representatives.

That night, Harding sent telegrams to Inaugural Chairman McLean and to the joint congressional Inaugural Committee. He sensed, as he said at the time, that the people at large opposed a gala inauguration, even though the funds for the celebration would come, as normally, from the Inaugural Committee, not the federal government. "I beg respectfully to suggest to your committee," Harding wired to McLean, "the complete abandonment of all plans for an inaugural celebration."

"Poor Ned!" his wife wrote. "I think he never had worked so hard to develop any project."

Harding himself had not wanted to cancel the celebration, but he did not suggest that in his telegrams. *I wish you and your committee to know that the impression of extravagant expenditures and excessive cost would make me a very unhappy participant,* he stated. *It will be most pleasing to me to be simply sworn in, speak briefly my plight of faith to the country and turn at once to the work which will be calling.*

The Congressional Inaugural Committee promptly notified him that the ceremony on the East Portico of the Capitol had been cancelled and that he would take the oath in the simplest of ceremonies in the Senate chamber. Harding quickly let the committee know that, in this, it had gone too far: he would like the swearing-in ceremony at the Capitol in the usual way.

Chairman McLean had no choice but to carry out Harding's request. He sent this word to all those already active in the plans: "The inaugural organization, following the wishes of President-elect Harding, will immediately cease to function." From his home in Northampton, Massachusetts, Vice President-elect Coolidge issued a statement supporting Harding's decision: *I am in entire harmony with the expressed wishes of Senator Harding to have the inaugural ceremonies simple and free from extravagance. I feel sure that Senator Harding's judgment is correct and will meet with general approbation. I can see no other position that he could take when the government is attempting to reduce extravagance.* The difference between Harding and Coolidge was that Coolidge really meant what he said.

From his Inaugural Committee headquarters at the New Willard Hotel, McLean issued a printed card confirming what he had already spoken: *In compliance with the expressed wishes of President-elect Warren G. Harding all ceremonies, including parade, etc., attending the inauguration of the President and Vice-President on March 4, 1921, be abandoned, it has been determined by this committee to cancel all arrangements of every character for that function.* One of the arrangements thus cancelled were the plans to strike inaugural medals.

The committee had proceeded as usual in such matters, and had arranged again with R. Harris & Company of Washington to produce these medals. The Harris company's engraver, Darrel C. Crain, made the design: it was a dramatic portrait of the President-elect.

Harding's formal request and McLean's repeated announcements seemed to bring all inauguration festivities to an end. In fact, the parade was cancelled and so

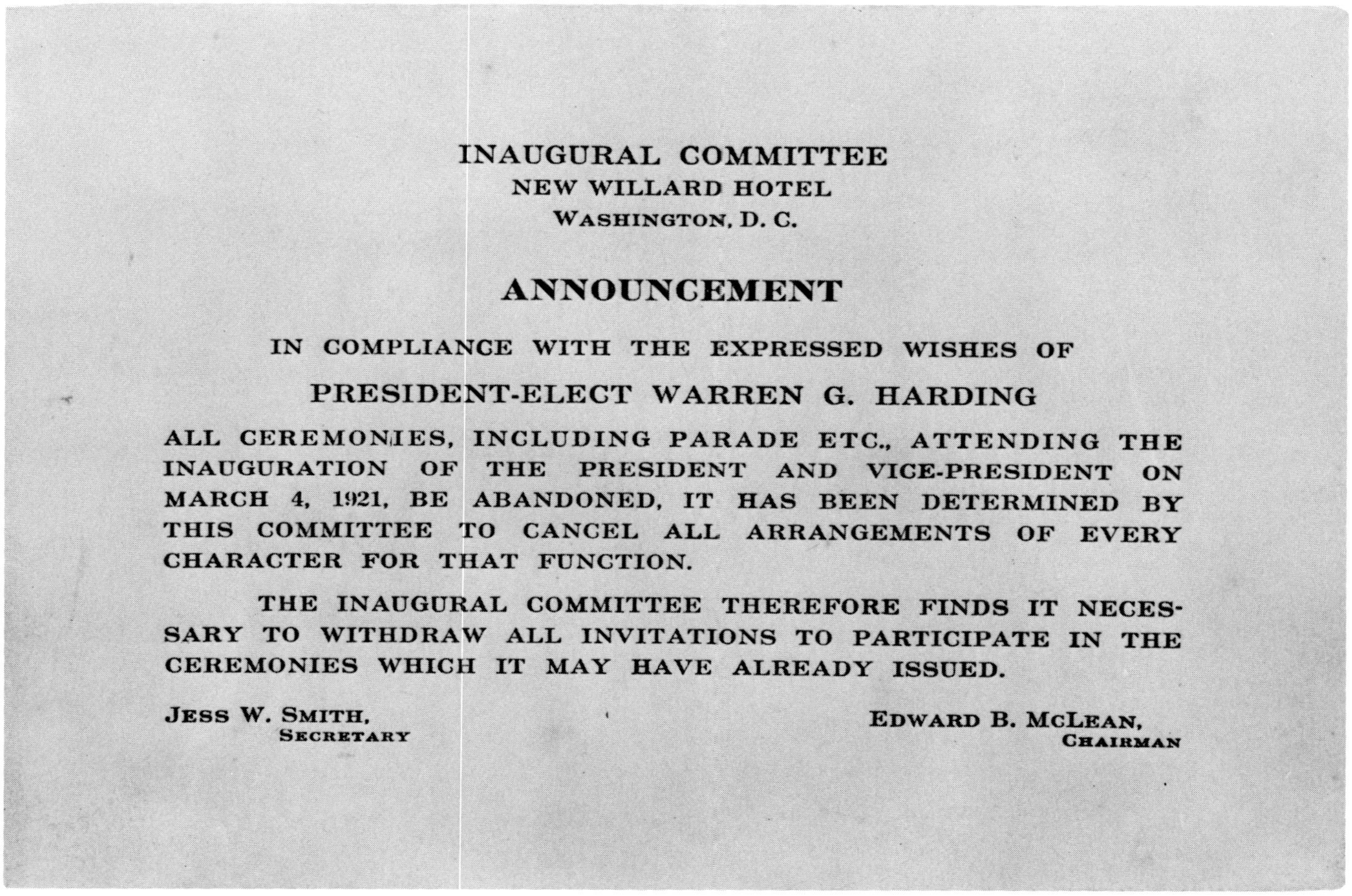

INAUGURAL COMMITTEE
NEW WILLARD HOTEL
WASHINGTON, D. C.

ANNOUNCEMENT

IN COMPLIANCE WITH THE EXPRESSED WISHES OF

PRESIDENT-ELECT WARREN G. HARDING

ALL CEREMONIES, INCLUDING PARADE ETC., ATTENDING THE INAUGURATION OF THE PRESIDENT AND VICE-PRESIDENT ON MARCH 4, 1921, BE ABANDONED, IT HAS BEEN DETERMINED BY THIS COMMITTEE TO CANCEL ALL ARRANGEMENTS OF EVERY CHARACTER FOR THAT FUNCTION.

THE INAUGURAL COMMITTEE THEREFORE FINDS IT NECESSARY TO WITHDRAW ALL INVITATIONS TO PARTICIPATE IN THE CEREMONIES WHICH IT MAY HAVE ALREADY ISSUED.

JESS W. SMITH,
SECRETARY

EDWARD B. McLEAN,
CHAIRMAN

Card issued by Chairman McLean
cancelling Harding inaugural festivities
Private collection

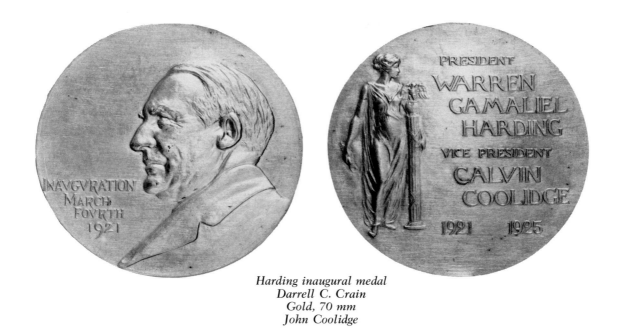

Harding inaugural medal
Darrell C. Crain
Gold, 70 mm
John Coolidge

was the fireworks display. But those in Washington knew that Harding had been pressured into making his request, and they did not feel bound by it. Under the auspices of Mrs. John Allan Dougherty, a leader in child welfare work in Washington, a charity ball was held, with Vice President Coolidge and his wife as the honored guests. An inaugural concert was also held that night.

"When the plans for an Inaugural Ball were abandoned," Mrs. McLean reported, "we determined that the McLeans would provide a celebration anyhow, and pay the bills without regard to pennypinching Senators." Before the charity ball, the McLeans gave an opulent dinner in their home. They set three tables, two in gold service, each a hundred feet long. To the dinner they invited, among others, the members-designate of Harding's cabinet, the justices of the Supreme Court, and, as guest of honor, Vice President Coolidge.

Similarly, and without formal acknowledgement, the Inaugural Committee had the Harris Company strike an inaugural medal in gold for President Harding and another for Vice President Coolidge. The gold medal given to Coolidge was found in 1975 among his effects in the attic of his only surviving son, John Coolidge. The Washington company also struck replicas of the medal in silver and bronze, but as its records were discarded, there are no figures on how many of these were struck. At least four of the Harding medals in silver are known. The bronze is the scarcest of all presidential inaugural medals, appearing rarely in numismatic circles. Perhaps fewer than sixty of them were struck.

Apparently, the company sold the Harding medals in silver or bronze to those who wanted to buy them. At least one Washington building contractor, active in Republican local politics, purchased several of each to give to business and political associates.

Because a few Washingtonians did buy these medals, and because Chairman McLean and others in charge of the aborted celebration refused to deny to President Harding and Vice President Coolidge gold inaugural medals, the tradition barely managed to survive in 1921. Whether McLean himself received a Harding gold inaugural medal, as Inaugural Committee chairmen had before him, is not known.

Probably he did. His successor was given one four years later, at a time of even greater austerity.

The Harris Company used the sensitive portrait of Harding again that year in a token struck for the Keller Mechanical Engraving Company for its twenty-fifth anniversary. The token carries only the initials "KME," not the name of the company.

Harding token struck for the
Keller Mechanical Engraving Company's twenty-fifth anniversary
Bronze, 34 × 27 mm
Private collection

WGH	1921	1	gold	(70 mm)	2, possibly 3
WGH	1921	2	silver	(70 mm)	4 known
WGH	1921	3	bronze	(70 mm)	unknown, possibly less than 60

CALVIN
COOLIDGE
1925

In 1923, on the death of President Harding, Calvin Coolidge succeeded to the presidency, and in the following year he won the presidential election by a landslide. His popularity was difficult to fathom. A man of chilling temperament, Coolidge was so prim that he would go trout fishing in a business suit with vest and tie, wearing a fedora hat. His pinched features inspired Alice Roosevelt Longworth, President Theodore Roosevelt's daughter, to say that he looked like he had been weaned on a pickle. When, four years before, Coolidge had endorsed President Harding's decision to cancel the official festivities, he had only stated his real sense of the proprieties. His years in the White House were a time of gentility, propriety, official silence, and an austerity that amounted to stinginess. He did not look kindly on the wasteful foolishness of an inauguration celebration, not even his own.

Those anxious to conduct an appropriate celebration were confronted by the President's own genuine hostility. After leaving the White House in 1929, Coolidge wrote his autobiography, and in it he expressed his distaste for ostentation: *It was my desire to maintain about the White House as far as possible an attitude of simplicity and not engage in anything that had an air of pretentious display. That was my conception of the great office. It carries sufficient powers within itself, so that it does not require any of the outward trappings of pomp and splendor for the purpose of creating an impression. It has a dignity of its own which makes it self-sufficient.* In short, President Coolidge wanted no fuss made about him taking the oath as President on March 4, 1925.

All the same, an Inaugural Committee was formed by the citizenry of Washington, and William T. Galliher, owner of a Washington lumberyard, was named chairman. This committee did what it could to celebrate Coolidge's inauguration in the traditional way, despite his continuing restraints on their activities. The *Washington Evening Star* reported that the ceremonies were "almost severely simple, all suggestion of pomp and panoply having been vetoed by the President himself." The newspaper reported, however, that "by its very simplicity the entire program was strikingly impressive and entirely befitting the administration he had established." The *Commonweal* found that Coolidge had received considerable praise for "cutting off all the decorative features" of his inauguration but, it also reported, "There has been little or no published dissent, though a good deal of regret, if not exactly censure, is currently expressed in private circles."

Coolidge restricted the size of the inaugural parade and declined to allow an official inaugural ball. Again, however, a charity ball was held on the night of the inauguration, under the sponsorship of a committee headed by Mrs. John Allan Dougherty, and the affair had all the markings of an inaugural ball except for the presence of the President and his wife. Vice President Charles Dawes and his wife did attend, as did the state governors in town for the occasion. The committee sold some four thousand tickets to this ball, and the excess funds, some $30,000, were given to children's charities and to a fund for firemen's widows and orphans.

The Inaugural Committee, limited as it was by President Coolidge, did not receive the revenues normal to a full-scale inaugural celebration. It received some funds from sales of tickets to the inaugural concert. No funds at all, of course, were available from the charity ball. The committee could not afford to restore the traditional practice of presenting a medal to each of its members. All the same, it did have some funds available, and it made the most of them.

The committee ordered special inaugural badges, complete with an attached medal bearing President Coolidge's portrait, quite similar to those for the 1889, 1893, and 1897 inaugurations. These were distributed to those working on the celebration. The medals were so designed that they could be detached from the ribbons and used as charms. The committee, moreover, authorized an inaugural medal to be struck for the President and Vice President.

Coolidge Inaugural Committee badge
Bronze, 28 mm
Private collection

Darrell C. Crain, who as the engraver for R. Harris & Company in Washington had designed the inaugural medals for Woodrow Wilson in 1917 and for Warren Harding in 1921, had by now organized his own partnership, Pearson & Crain, and he probably sought the contract for the Coolidge inaugural medal. His firm did receive the contract, and Crain, by his own account, designed the medal chosen. As he later wrote, he had by now "considerable experience in producing fine medals." The models for the obverse and reverse were executed by Julio Kilényi (1885–1958), a prominent sculptor with a growing national reputation, and the medals produced bear his name. For this, Kilényi received a fee of $150.

Pearson & Crain had no facilities for striking medals, and they subcontracted the order to the Medallic Art Company of New York City. This was the first presidential inaugural medal struck by the Medallic Art Company, a firm which, in later years, nearly monopolized this special field.

Curiously, the Coolidge inaugural medals appear to have been made as an afterthought. Pearson & Crain did not give its order to the Medallic Art Company until May 11, 1925, more than two months after the inauguration. On that date, the Washington firm ordered two medals struck in gold, one for President Coolidge, the other for Vice President Dawes, and seventy-five struck in bronze, presumably for distribution among the leaders of the Inaugural Committee.

The gold medals, by the still extant order sheet, were to be in eighteen-karat gold, two-and-three-quarters inches in diameter, "reproduced from models that will be submitted to you [the Inaugural Committee] for final approval." The obverse, as usual, was to have the portrait of the President, and the reverse would be a design

Coolidge inaugural medal
Julio Kilényi after Darrell C. Crain
Gold, 70 mm
John Coolidge

already sketched by Crain, a modification of the presidential seal. These gold medals were housed in black morocco leather cases with dark green linings.

Three days after the Medallic Art Company received this order, on May 14, Pearson & Crain sent in another order for three more medals: another in gold and two in silver. The gold medal was for Chairman Galliher. It is not known who received those in silver. The Medallic Art Company charged $118.47 for each of the gold medals, plus Kilényi's fee, as the private mint had commissioned him. The firm charged $6.95 for each of the silver medals. They had the medals ready by June 15.

Next to the Harding, the Coolidge is the rarest of presidential inaugural medals. The Coolidge inaugural badge also is exceedingly rare. As in 1917 and in 1921, few inaugural medals were made in 1925 and, once again, the tradition barely survived. The Coolidge medal would be the last to depend on the Inaugural Committee's other resources. For the next inauguration, the financing of the medal would be radically changed, and in such a way that it could pay for itself.

Two years afterwards, the Medallic Art Company reused the Crain–Kilényi models of the Coolidge medal to strike a special medal for this President. It was to mark his honorary membership in the Union League of Philadelphia; more than three thousand copies were struck.

Medal struck when Coolidge became
an honorary member of the Union League of Philadelphia
Julio Kilényi and Darrell C. Crain
Bronze, 62 mm
Private collection

CC	1925	1	gold	(70 mm)	3
CC	1925	2	silver	(70 mm)	2
CC	1925	3	bronze	(70 mm)	75
CC	1925	4	bronze	(28 mm medal on badge)	unknown

HERBERT
HOOVER
1929

For different reasons, the inaugurations of 1917, 1921, and 1925 had been celebrated in less than exuberant style. In each case, there had been no official ball and only a nominal, somewhat truncated parade. Strapped for funds, the Inaugural Committees of these years had nothing to spare for such extravagances as giving away medals as souvenirs. Even so, the tradition of the President's medal had survived. Wilson, Harding, and Coolidge each had received a medal struck in gold, and so had their Vice Presidents. At each inauguration, at least some replicas of the medals had been struck in bronze. The inauguration of 1929 revivied the old traditions, including the official commitment to inaugural medals.

Shortly after the election of Herbert Hoover in November 1928, he let it be known that he had no objections to a full-scale celebration of the inauguration. He did ask that the ball, like those for Harding and Coolidge, remain a charity ball, but he had no personal or political problems with the other traditional ways of celebrating the inauguration. Lieutenant Colonel Ulysses S. Grant, 3rd, who had been named Chairman of the Inaugural Committee, was so informed, and he immediately undertook to organize a full-scale inauguration. Mrs. John Allan Dougherty agreed to organize another charity ball, as she had in 1921 and 1925, to be held on inauguration night. Hoover did not attend the ball, but his Vice President, Charles Curtis, did.

Chairman Grant met with a group of prominent Washington business and civic leaders, and with their help appointed the chairman of the subsidiary committees. They agreed to raise a Guarantee Fund of $100,000; it was oversubscribed by $12,000. They also agreed to other features of the traditional inauguration, but they felt as though they were beginning anew with some of these operations. Not since 1913 had a full-scale celebration been undertaken, and Grant's committee discovered that they suffered from, in his words, "the want of adequate definite information" on what past Inaugural Committees had actually done.

Grant appointed Julius Garfinckel, a local businessman, as chairman of the committee on medals and badges. As usual, Garfinckel had the choice of his committee colleagues. Among those he selected were Robert J. Grant, Director of the United States Mint, and Henry Kirke Bush-Brown, a Washington sculptor, now seventy-one years old. "Following the precedent set by previous inaugurations," Garfinckel stated, "we made immediate plans to give a gold medal of the same design each to Mr. Hoover and Mr. Curtis." Here, apparently unwittingly, Garfinckel did not carry out the full precedent set in former inaugurations. Since 1897, the Chairman of the Inaugural Committee, as well as the President and Vice President, had normally received inaugural medals in gold. Garfinckel's committee did not so provide the 1929 Chairman, and only rarely in the years after this did the Inaugural Committee Chairman receive the same gold medal.

Garfinckel's committee asked Bush-Brown, the sculptor on the committee, to make the Hoover inaugural medal. Bush-Brown accepted, asking only for a fee large enough to cover his expenses. He had no opportunity to model the portrait of the President-elect from life, but Hoover was not indifferent to his needs. Told that the Inaugural Committee had commissioned the usual inaugural medal, Hoover selected a photograph of himself for the artist to use, and asked his assistant, Lawrence Richey, to send it to Bush-Brown. "This," wrote Richey to Bush-Brown, "is Mr. Hoover's choice."

The artist, whose studio was only a few hundred yards from the White House, sketched designs for the obverse and reverse of the inaugural medal, and these he submitted to his fellow committee members for approval. Once they were approved, he returned to his studio and worked up the plaster models for each side of the medal. The portrait remarkably captured the rough-hewn vigor of the miner-engineer about to become President. A rugged individualist in temperament, as well as a rugged man physically, Hoover appeared in the portrait as a firm, steady man of great latent energy.

Hoover inaugural medal
Henry Kirke Bush-Brown
Gold, 70 mm
Herbert Hoover Presidential Library

The reverse, in the words of the medals committee's report, showed "the sculptor's conception of the outstanding achievements so far in the life of the President-elect." Bush-Brown himself wrote a detailed description of the reverse and what he intended with his design. The committee sent a copy of this to everyone purchasing one of the medals. The central portion of the reverse carried the names of the President and Vice President, and the eagle of the President's seal. Beneath this, Bush-Brown showed the book, *De Re Metallica* by Agricola, which Hoover and his wife had translated from Latin to English. The sculptor also used the emblems of mining, the pick and hammer, as well as the steam shovel, the mine head, and the mountains. "On the left," he wrote, "is the American Star of Hope, sending its blessed rays of Christian brotherly relief to the starving people of Europe. Mr. Hoover was the embodiment of this great service and this is the great reason why he is today the President-elect."

The artist received the photograph of the President on January 18, "quite in time," as he wrote back to Hoover's assistant, to be used for the medal. He had the medal done by February 23. To protect Bush-Brown's design and models, Chairman Garfinckel copyrighted the medal on behalf of the Inaugural Committee.

There was a curiosity on the reverse of the medal. In designing the eagle, Bush-Brown turned the eagle's head to its left, toward the talons grasping the arrows. Over the years a superstition had grown in Washington about the President's seal: if the eagle's head turned toward the olive branch, that prophesied a peaceful administration, but if it turned toward the arrows, that meant a troublesome, warlike administration.

Garfinckel and his committee colleagues would not be satisfied with just striking the two medals in gold. They wanted as well to make replicas available to others, and they came up with an idea that permanently altered the history of presidential inaugural medals: they would sell them. "As the same models could be used," Garfinckel explained, "the idea evolved to have bronze medals, replicas of the gold, struck off and to sell these as the official souvenirs of the occasion."

"This was something new," Garfinckel said, "and . . . had never been tried in connection with a previous inauguration." What this medals committee really invented was a plan to have the inaugural medals pay for themselves. The members had found a way to place this tradition on a self-sustaining basis, without reference to the condition of the country or the foibles of the man elected President. Whether depression or prosperity, war or peace, the medals could be sold and thereby continued. No longer would their fate depend on the ability of the Inaugural Committee to turn a financial profit. The committee's decision, so simple and reasonable, utterly changed the very nature of these inaugural medals. For the next two decades, they would be struck on a self-supporting basis. Thereafter, they would become a major financial operation of the Inaugural Committees and a principal means of defraying the whole cost of future celebrations. Indeed, in time, the medals that had once depended on the financial success of the inauguration ceremonies ironically themselves became the vehicle of making the inauguration a financial success.

The decision to sell the medals, and thereby to have them pay for themselves, was not the only new ground cut by this medals committee. The members also decided to have them struck by the United States Mint, doubtlessly because the Director of the Mint, Robert J. Grant, was serving as a member of the medals committee. A mining engineer and long-time gold miner prior to his government service, he knew intimately the intricate details of striking medals. He had been Director of the Mint since 1923, and before that, superintendent of the Mint at Denver.

There were advantages and disadvantages to awarding the contract for the medals to the United States Mint instead of a private mint or medal company. For those inexperienced in drafting medal contracts, the Mint gave assurance that its fees were not exorbitant: only the cost of making the medals, although that cost included a complex formula covering part of the Mint's overhead. The reason for charging just the cost was obvious: the Mint did not want to appear to be in the business of making profits on private contracts. Under the law then in effect, the Mint could only strike medals for private contract with dies provided by the contractor: it had no legal authority to make the dies on a private contract.

The medals committee members had not at first known that government regulation but, confronted with it, they sought a private firm to fashion the dies from Bush-Brown's plaster models. They approached the Medallic Art Company of New York, and at first that firm refused to make the dies unless the committee awarded it the contract to strike the medals too. Medallic Art had struck the Coolidge inaugural medals four years before. Finally the company's officials agreed to make the dies for the Mint.

With these arrangements, the committee ordered five hundred medals. The committee members, of course, could not act on their own in a financial matter of this import, and they consulted with the members of the parent Inaugural Committee. That body approved the plan to sell the medals instead of giving them away. Chairman Grant, however, questioned whether five hundred medals would be enough to satisfy demand. After all, many members of the Inaugural Committee would wish to buy them as mementos. At Grant's suggestion, the medals committee increased the order to a thousand. The Mint charged the medals committee 55 cents for each bronze medal and actually made 1,012, for a cost to the committee of $556.60.

The committee tried its best to sell as many medals as possible. It guaranteed that only a thousand would be struck and suggested that at some time they would be valuable. The committee planned as well to have the dies destroyed, as assurance that no more than the allotted number would be made. It approached the local newspapers, three of which published free advertisements. As another part of its sales campaign, the medals committee persuaded the committee publishing the official program to include photographs of the medal's obverse and reverse with a notice stating that it could be purchased at the Willard Hotel. The notice stated that the medal was the "only official souvenir" of President Hoover's inauguration.

The sales program was more than successful. The committee disposed of all the medals, and Chairman Garfinckel wrote to the White House on March 14, ten days after the inauguration, that "We could sell many thousands more, but we told the public that only the thousand would be struck off and we think it is only fair to keep faith with the people."

The medals committee, plainly, had no intention of making money, but rather to do little more than pay production costs. The commercialization would come in later years.

The profit on the medals sold was $1,662.84. Far more significantly, the committee had found a way to perpetuate the tradition of inaugural medals and had found, as well, a potential resource for revenue that would produce, for one future Inaugural Committee, a net profit of $1,000,000.

| HCH | 1929 | 1 | gold | (70 mm) | 2 |
| HCH | 1929 | 2 | bronze | (70 mm) | 1,012 |

88

FRANKLIN D. ROOSEVELT
1933

In 1932, the United States suffered in the depths of a trying depression, and that November the American voters elected Franklin Delano Roosevelt, the Governor of New York, as President of the United States. The Democrats would command the national government for the first time since Woodrow Wilson had left the White House in 1921. The inauguration to come in March 1933 would be a time of celebration by the Democrats and certainly a financial success. President-elect Roosevelt asked an old friend, Admiral Cary T. Grayson, to serve as Chairman of the Inaugural Committee, and Grayson proceeded to name the chairmen of the usual committees. There was no doubt what was afoot: this would be a return to the ceremonies of old, including an official inaugural ball. Grayson named a man familiar with Washington to be chairman of the medals committee, Robert W. Woolley.

Woolley, born in 1871, had a many-sided career. A journalist, a lawyer, a government bureaucrat, a congressional investigator at various times, he had served for almost two years (1915–1916) as Director of the United States Mint in President Wilson's first administration. He had quit that post to become director of publicity of the Democratic National Committee, and it was he who had coined Wilson's winning campaign slogan that year: "He kept us out of war." He had known Franklin Roosevelt from those years with President Wilson. His experience at the Mint gave him special credentials to chair the inaugural medals committee.

Chairman Woolley had no plan other than to follow the precedent set by the 1929 medals committee: commission a sculptor to design the medal, have it struck by the United States Mint, and then sell replicas to the general public. Despite the enthusiasm of the Democrats, despite the confidence that the full-scale inauguration ceremonies would prove a financial success, Woolley and his committee apparently did not even consider returning to the old-style system of giving these medals to the inauguration workers. Significantly, he also named to his committee the Director of the Mint, Robert J. Grant, who had served on it in 1929.

Chairman Woolley, however, had his own decided views on one matter: the inaugural medal for his friend, the President-elect, must be a work of art. As a former Director of the United States Mint, he was familiar enough with the commercial vapidities that had passed for medallic art in his time. Woolley wanted a top-flight artist to create a truly memorable work. He and his fellow committee members treated the matter of choosing a sculptor with care. By Woolley's own account, they studied the works of a half dozen artists. They consulted with several authorities on medals and medalists. Only then did they decide to ask Paul Manship to take the commission. Manship, forty-seven years old, was then at the height of his powers, with a worldwide reputation. "He has long been recognized as having few peers in this profession," Woolley later reported. "Mr. Manship accepted the commission with enthusiasm, agreeing that his compensation should be relatively a nominal one."

Manship agreed to a fee of $500. For him, this was a special assignment, and he felt the honor of it. He had known Roosevelt for many years, as early as 1919, when he had acted as advisor for Roosevelt, then Assistant Secretary of the Navy, about a desired change in the design of the Navy's Medal of Honor. As fellow New Yorkers, the Manships had called on Governor Roosevelt in Albany; and Mrs. Roosevelt's return visit to the Manship home in New York City for tea one afternoon shortly thereafter was an occasion not forgotten in the Manship family nearly half a century later. "The Roosevelts," said Paul Manship's daughter Pauline, "were very civilized people."

The sculptor's admiration for the President-elect had to inspire him to do his best, and Roosevelt's awareness of Manship's talent made him more than cooperative. He was delighted that his friend Manship had been chosen, and he sat twice for him. At the conclusion of the second sitting, Manship had his portrait completed. He had modelled Roosevelt in left profile, in a bold relief higher than in any previous inaugural medal or in any yet to follow. Chairman Woolley had wanted a work of artistic merit, and Manship could count on him to protect the bold-relief portrait from the intruding complaints of those who wanted to reduce it and cut costs. The portrait would take twelve strikes from the great hydraulic presses at the United States Mint to bring out its final details. A master of bold relief, Manship had not hesitated to use his mastery on this portrait of his admired friend about to venture on a presidential career.

As Manship sculpted the portrait, Roosevelt asked him about his plans for the reverse of the medal. Needless to say, Manship was more than anxious for him to make suggestions. Roosevelt had a natural affinity for the sea, for the Navy. He wanted a naval theme for the reverse, and suggested that Manship use an old print from his own collection, of the U.S.S. *Constitution,* the fabled "Old Ironsides," commissioned in 1798. He also asked Manship to use, around the rim of the reverse, Longfellow's famous lines: "Thou too sail on, O Ship of State, Sail on, O Union, strong and great."

Roosevelt had offered a theme, and the sculptor leaped to work upon it his special prowess. "Old Ironsides" in full sail became the central figure of the reverse, with the poet's gallant words inscribed as the border. Beneath the ship, Manship modelled a winged woman to symbolize the "Ship of State" of the present day. The models were completed in plaster by early February, and the artist exhibited them at his studio in New York City on February 4. He had completed the portrait of Roosevelt, he told the press, in two days, after two sittings. "The reverse was suggested by Mr. Roosevelt himself," Mr. Manship said, "and is reminiscent of his hobby. I had thought of something perfectly conventional, Columbia and her eagle, you know, but I like this much better."

Chairman Woolley and his fellow committee members obviously were pleased with Manship's work. It had met Woolley's hope to produce a genuine work of art, and he proposed to have it struck in no less than 2,500 copies. "This seemed to be warranted," Woolley later argued, "because the medal, as designed, was regarded as an unusual artistic triumph and because a very large attendance at the inaugural was then anticipated." He believed that the occasion of the inauguration and the merit of Manship's artistry would assure the medal's success with the purchasing public. His committee decided to strike this medal at a full three-inch diameter to accent the artistic merit of the design.

Early in January, the committee had contacted the Superintendent of the

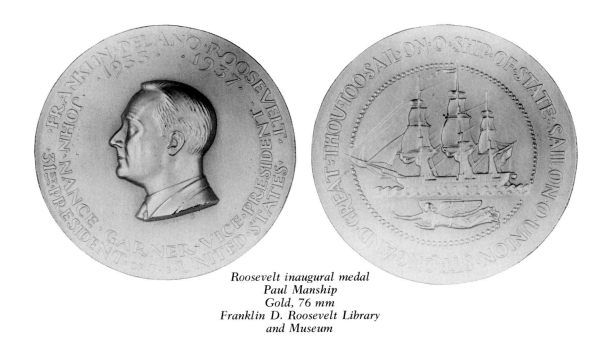

Roosevelt inaugural medal
Paul Manship
Gold, 76 mm
Franklin D. Roosevelt Library
and Museum

United States Mint at Philadelphia to request a quotation for striking these inaugural medals. That official promptly referred the decision to his headquarters in Washington. The director's office had no objections to quoting prices for presidential inaugural medals, but cautioned the superintendent: "It is understood that the Mint will make this quotation only on request and not undertake to seek this business. It is also understood that the dies for this medal will be supplied to you."

Woolley contacted the Medallic Art Company to make the dies, as the medals committee chairman in 1929 had done. The firm agreed to make the dies, but now wanted to make these medals even more than it had four years earlier. Like most companies, Medallic Art had been badly hurt by the national depression: it needed the business.

The Medallic Art Company could not match the United States Mint's quotation to strike this unusually high-relief medal, three inches in diameter, in bronze, for 85 cents each. The private firm did make two sets of dies for the obverse and reverse, and, in a further effort to win the contract, struck fifty replicas on its own presses. The company used a thicker planchet than the United States Mint later used, and gave the medal a slightly rounded edge, as against the Mint's sharper rim. Moreover, Medallic Art gave these replicas a dark brown torch finish, quite different from the Mint's high golden bronze finish, and stamped the rim with its name. Some it gold-plated. The company could claim that it was merely testing the dies, but its real motive was to win the contract. "We wanted the business," one employee of the firm would later state. The effect of the private firm's action was to make a numismatic rarity, an inaugural medal distinctly different from that ordered from the United States Mint, even though struck from the same dies.

Striking these medals delayed delivery of the dies to the Mint at Philadelphia. On February 16, a full dozen days after Manship had exhibited his plaster models, the Director of the Mint sent to Medallic Art Company what amounted to an order to ship the dies "as quickly as possible." Not until five days later did the company reply that both sets of dies had been sent.

In these final days of February, the national economy underwent a financial

91

crisis that enormously compounded the already critical depression. Many who had intended to come to Washington for the inauguration cancelled their plans. The medals committee therefore cut back its order at the Mint to 1,500. These the committee had already priced at $2.50 each, the same price as the inaugural medal in 1929, even though it had cost more to make. As his first major action as President, Roosevelt closed the banks, to prevent many of them from being foreclosed, and that further inhibited sales of the medals.

Some weeks after the inauguration, Chairman Woolley visited President Roosevelt at the White House and told him that, regretfully, his committee had not been able to sell all of the inaugural medals struck. Why not, Roosevelt asked.

"You closed the banks," Woolley answered, "and I wouldn't take checks."

The President burst out laughing.

Woolley told him that the committee had sold a thousand medals and that five hundred were left over. More precisely, the records show that he actually sold only 902. A few had been lost, and there were still 581 unsold. What to do with these became a problem for Woolley and Admiral Grayson, the Inaugural Committee chairman. The accountant for the inauguration listed them as unsaleable, with a value, for all 581 of them, of just $1.00. Woolley so treated them. Later, with President Roosevelt's permission, he sent scores of them as gifts to libraries, art galleries, and colleges. The rest were put in storage and forgotten. More than forty years later, a large number were discovered in the estate of Admiral Grayson.

At one point, the committee considered striking ten inaugural medals in silver for President Roosevelt's new cabinet. That apparently was not done. Chairman Woolley reported that only two were struck in silver, one presumably for himself, the other for Admiral Grayson. In recent years, four silver medals have been located, but the United States Mint has found no surviving records to indicate just how many were struck in silver. As in 1929, the committee directed that two medals be struck in gold, one for President Roosevelt, the other for Vice President John Nance Garner. These were presented by Admiral Grayson and Chairman Woolley.

Despite the economic disaster that engulfed the country at that time, the inauguration itself proved a financial success. The Guarantee Fund was repaid in full, and the Inaugural Committee had $59,000 to distribute to local charities. The inaugural medals had not only paid for themselves, but the medals committee was able to turn over to the general fund a small profit. Using the same accounting methods as used in 1929, that profit was $639.73. In 1929, a time of national prosperity, the experiment had been tried to continue the tradition of presidential inaugural medals by public sale, and it had worked. In 1933, a time of desperate economic depression, that tradition had survived.

FDR	1933	1	gold	(76 mm)	2
FDR	1933	2	silver	(76 mm)	4 known
FDR	1933	3	bronze	(76 mm)	1,500
FDR	1933	4	bronze, Medallic Art	(76 mm)	50

FRANKLIN D.
ROOSEVELT
1937

In November 1936, President Roosevelt resoundingly won a second term in the White House, sweeping the electoral votes of every state in the Union except Vermont and Maine. After the election, he left Washington on a goodwill visit to Argentina, Brazil, and Uruguay, not returning until December 15. His absence from the country complicated the preparations for his second inauguration. Admiral Grayson, again chosen as Chairman of the Inaugural Committee, cabled to the President on December 11, asking him to decide how "extensive" a celebration the inauguration should be. "Twenty-five million contented countrymen will come and create city chaos if you encourage them," Grayson cabled to Roosevelt. "You recall Jackson's inauguration. However, I am brave and always at your service."

Since the last inauguration, in 1933, the United States Constitution had been amended, altering the inauguration date. In 1937, for the first time, the President would take the oath of office on January 20, a full six weeks earlier than in previous years. This meant that all the preparations had to be that much speeded to completion, and it raised a special problem for creating a new inaugural medal. The President ·was away, unavailable to pose for any sculptor the Inaugural Committee might select. There was little time to make the medal, even if a model could be designed and sculpted. Reluctantly, Admiral Grayson and his friend Robert Woolley, whom Grayson had again named as chairman of the medals and badges committee, decided that they would have to forego an inaugural medal this year. Obviously, they felt they had no choice in the matter.

Yet a curious chance changed their minds. On December 18, scarcely a month from inauguration, a Washington sculptor and painter, Joseph Anthony Atchison (1895–1967), called at the headquarters of the Inaugural Committee. Atchison, forty-one years old, had modelled a portrait of President Roosevelt for use as an inaugural medal. He had brought it with him to the committee. He had not, of course, seen the President; he had worked from a photograph. He had received no encouragement from the committee. Indeed, when he presented the model, committee officials told him that there would be no medal for this inauguration. Atchison had completed only the obverse, the portrait of Roosevelt. He left the model with the committee, despite the discouraging information he had received.

It was thus that Atchison's model came to the attention of Chairman Woolley. He was impressed, and he sent word to the artist to meet him at Chairman Grayson's office on Tuesday, December 22. Grayson immediately liked Atchison's portrait. How long, he asked the sculptor, would he need to make the reverse? Could this be a portrait of Vice President John Nance Garner? Atchison was more than pleased, more than anxious, to have his work accepted. He worked late into the night, and the next day he had the reverse for the medal, with Garner's portrait, ready for the committee.

Roosevelt inaugural medal
Joseph Anthony Atchison
Gold, 76 mm
Franklin D. Roosevelt Library
and Museum

That day, with Admiral Grayson's authority, the medals committee approved Atchison's model, and the next day, Christmas Eve, the committee's officials took the model to the White House for President Roosevelt's approval. Later that day, the model was sent to the Medallic Art Company in New York City, for that firm to make the dies as quickly as possible.

Woolley had miscalculated in 1933 on the number of medals made. He ordered too many. He made no such mistake now. He asked the Philadelphia Mint how quickly it could strike a thousand replicas of Atchison's medal; he knew that the dies would take time. The Mint officials told Woolley that if the dies reached Philadelphia by January 10, as expected, they would be forced to order overtime to complete the thousand medals by January 20. They could produce only about fifty medals a day unless they ordered overtime work. Even if they received the dies by January 4, they would need overtime to complete the order.

Woolley, himself a former Director of the United States Mint, knew he had to make other arrangements. He consulted with officials of the Medallic Art Company, who told him they would charge $320 for the dies, and $850 to strike a thousand replicas in bronze. Chairman Woolley agreed. As soon as the dies were ready, Medallic Art struck two copies of the medal and gave them the same dark brown torch patina used on the fifty inaugural medals it had made from the 1933 dies. Clyde C. Trees, president of the company, promptly sent these samples to Chairman Woolley. It was January 14, less than a week before inauguration day. Four days later, the company had the rest of the order on its way to Washington, in time for the inauguration. "Of course, this was a 'thank you mam' job," Trees wrote to Woolley. "No firm could make money on these prices. Just the same we were glad to do it, and were pleased to have the association with you all."

Medallic Art had struck two medals in gold, for President Roosevelt and Vice President Garner; two in silver, for Admiral Grayson and Woolley; two in the special dark patina; and 1,006 in golden bronze finish (two for the sculptor as a courtesy to him and four for its archives). The medals committee paid Atchison $300, and later

Chairman Woolley gave him one of the dark patina medals, keeping the other one for himself.

Before the medals had arrived, Woolley and his committee members were busy trying to sell them. The price was $2.50 each, and in the days of the inauguration celebration, they sold 732. These were still difficult days economically for many Americans and, despite the enthusiasm of many for Roosevelt, there were not enough buyers. It was a repetition of the 1933 predicament.

In late March, Woolley received a letter from a Washington coin dealer, Harry X. Boosel, who had learned that all the medals had not been sold. Boosel offered to buy them for $1.50 apiece, or to advise Woolley how to sell them for a fee of $100. Woolley consulted with Chairman Grayson, and the two agreed to sell the medals to Boosel. The dealer, however, had not originally realized that so many of the medals— 268 of them—had not sold. He agreed to buy 150 of these for the price he had earlier offered, $1.50 each. The remaining medals, 118 of them, Woolley put in his office safe. On April 25, 1938, he wrote to President Roosevelt to report that he still had these unsold inaugural medals: *Four years ago, you may recall, there was also a surplusage. I believe you directed that they be donated to libraries, art museums, etc. It occurs to me that you would like to give similar instructions in the present instance.* President Roosevelt replied on April 27, agreeing to Woolley's suggestion. "If you have any to spare," he wrote, "I should much like to have ten or twelve of them for members of my family—younger generation—who did not get any." Woolley, of course, sent them as requested. He, however, did not carry out Roosevelt's instructions to distribute the others to libraries and art museums. He had lost his 1933 list of these institutions, and he forgot about the matter.

Boosel, the Washington coin dealer, had little success selling the replicas that he had bought from the committee, despite his early confidence. He sold some at the start and then an occasional medal now and then. In 1968, more than thirty years later, he still had more than fifty. That year, he sold fifty-one of them back to the Medallic Art Company for $3.00 each; Medallic sold them to another firm at $6.00 each; and the medals finally reached collectors.

In the months that followed the United States' entry into World War II, Americans were asked to sacrifice as much as they could to the war effort. One commodity, in such short supply that the government was forced to change the American coinage, was copper. Americans were asked to donate whatever copper they could find, and this appeal reminded Woolley that he still had those unsold 1937 inaugural medals in his office safe. He decided he had best write to President Roosevelt about them. It was July 1942. *Longer ago than I like to admit I wrote you I had in my safe about a hundred unsold 1937 inaugural medals and suggested that these be distributed among a like number of museums and libraries. Just as was done with the 1933 surplus. You kindly endorsed the plan. Unfortunately the list previously used was lost and I never found time to prepare a new one. So I still have the medals.*

With your approval I shall, on behalf of the erstwhile Inaugural Committee, contribute these beautiful bronze discs to the copper pile for the war effort.

President Roosevelt replied to Woolley on July 8: *Dear Bob: I have your letter suggesting that the unsold 1937 Inaugural Medals be contributed to the copper pile for the war effort and I think it is a splendid idea. It has my approval. Very sincerely yours, FDR.*

Woolley did not send all of the 106 medals he still had to the copper pile. He retained about a dozen, but the rest, more than ninety, were melted down and destroyed.

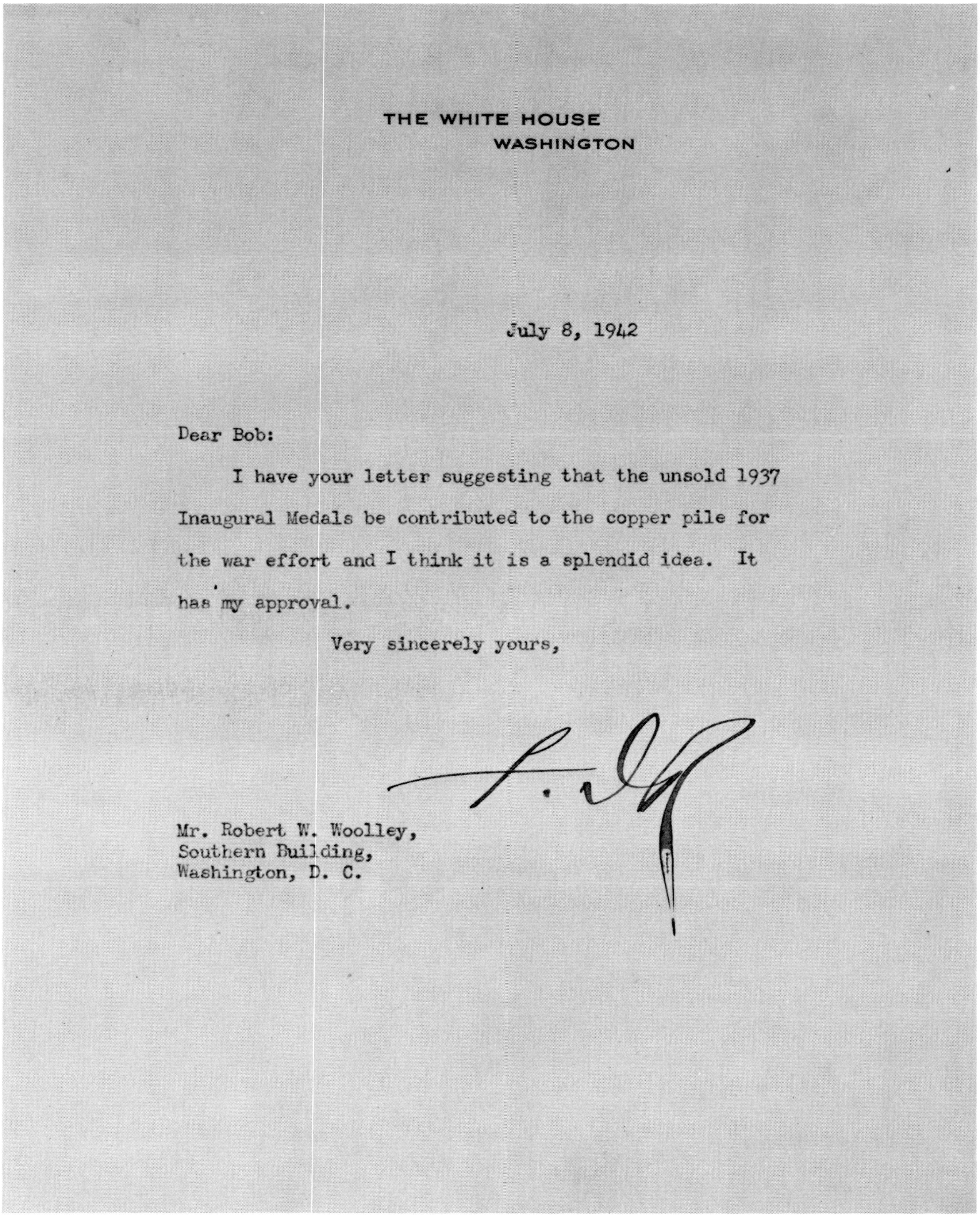

THE WHITE HOUSE
WASHINGTON

July 8, 1942

Dear Bob:

I have your letter suggesting that the unsold 1937 Inaugural Medals be contributed to the copper pile for the war effort and I think it is a splendid idea. It has my approval.

Very sincerely yours,

[signature]

Mr. Robert W. Woolley,
Southern Building,
Washington, D. C.

Letter, Roosevelt to Robert Woolley, July 8, 1942
Library of Congress

Police badge, first issued in 1937,
and produced for each subsequent inauguration.
This badge, No. 1, belonged to
Admiral Cary Grayson,
Chairman of the 1937 Inaugural Committee.
Private collection

FDR	1937	1	gold	(76 mm)	2
FDR	1937	2	silver	(76 mm)	2
FDR	1937	3	bronze	(76 mm)	1,006*
FDR	1937	4	bronze dark torch finish	(76 mm)	2

* Of these, with President Roosevelt's permission, more than ninety were contributed to the war effort and destroyed.

FRANKLIN D. ROOSEVELT
1941

When Franklin Delano Roosevelt won reelection to a third term in 1940, he broke a tradition as old as the American republic, which made his inauguration on January 20, 1941, equally unprecedented. Roosevelt asked his friend Joseph E. Davies, a long-time diplomat, to "take on immediately the Chairmanship of his Inaugural Committee," as Davies phrased it in his private diary, "which I was proud to do." Admiral Grayson, who had been chairman of the 1933 and 1937 inaugurations, had died in 1938.

Davies knew the tradition of inaugural medals, and he promptly sought help from Robert Woolley, chairman of the medals committee for the previous two inaugurations. Woolley had no stomach to take on the frustrating chore again. "I don't know as I blame you," Davies told him, after hearing his reasons. Woolley, however, did agree to write an extensive memorandum offering suggestions about the new medal. Davies then asked Mrs. Nellie Tayloe Ross to serve as chairman of the medals committee. The first woman elected governor of a state, Wyoming, Mrs. Ross had served since 1933 as Director of the United States Mint. In 1937, she had been a member of the inaugural medals committee, and she readily accepted Davies's invitation to chair the 1941 committee.

In preliminary discussions with President Roosevelt about his third inauguration, Chairman Davies sought his views on its various aspects. Roosevelt knew, of course, that neither the 1933 nor the 1937 medals had sold well. To Davies he indicated his feeling that they had been "quite costly." Implicitly, he was suggesting that the 1941 medal be sold at a much lower price. Chairman Davies relayed the President's wishes to Mrs. Ross. The 1933 and 1937 medals had sold for $2.50 each. They had been large, three inches in diameter. To meet the President's wishes, the inaugural officials decided that the 1941 medal would be priced at just $1.00, plus 10 cents for postage if ordered by mail. That price dictated a reduction in size, and the committee decided on a medal one-and-five-eighths inches in diameter. To help expedite matters, President Roosevelt authorized the Mint to strike the 1941 medals, on orders from the Inaugural Committee, as had been done in 1929 and 1933.

As so often in the past, there were delays in deciding essential questions about the medal, and then a rush resembling panic to produce them by inauguration day. Not until December 26, the day after Christmas, was the sculptor selected. Chairman Davies had gone to Florida for the holidays, and Mrs. Ross telephoned him there. Davies suggested Jo Davidson, a renowned sculptor then at the height of his powers and his fame, for the commission. Davidson had spent most of his career in France, but he was a personal friend of both Davies and the President. Indeed, he had a cordial friendship with Roosevelt. Four years before this, Roosevelt had given him no less than sixteen sittings for his now famous bust and, in their time together, the two men had become friends.

As soon as Mrs. Ross finished her conversation with Davies, she telephoned

Nellie Tayloe Ross, Director of the United States Mint, served on four inaugural committees.
Here she is shown with Roosevelt.
Bradford Ross

Davidson at his new studios in rural Pennsylvania. In his memoirs, *Between Sittings,* Davidson remembered this call as coming from Ambassador Davies, probably because Mrs. Ross told the artist that she was calling him at Davies's suggestion. Mrs. Ross apologized for her "last-minute call" less than a month before inauguration day. Davidson nevertheless accepted the commission instantly. He felt honored; he charged no fee. He made no objections to the shortness of the time allowed, either, even though Mrs. Ross told him that the Mint would need a "minimum" of eighteen days to make the dies and strike the thousand medals in bronze that the Inaugural Committee intended to order. That meant, Mrs. Ross said, that Davidson had to complete his model by January 1—just six days away. "It was a rush job," Davidson wrote in his memoirs.

Every effort was made to save time. Mrs. Ross asked Davidson to model his portrait from a photograph of the Salisbury painting, Roosevelt's favorite portrait of himself. That same day, December 26, Mrs. Ross sent the photograph to Davidson by special courier in an automobile. Davidson was to design only the obverse of the medal, the portrait of the President. The reverse would be executed at the Mint in Philadelphia by its chief engraver, John Sinnock (1888–1947). To expedite matters further, Davidson was asked to make his portrait model only seven inches in diameter, considerably smaller than the ten or twelve inches, or even larger size, normally preferred by sculptors of medals. This was to shorten the time needed to cut the master die. Speed had become everything. "If you will inform me when the model is ready to leave your hands," Mrs. Ross wrote to Davidson, "I will have a messenger there to receive it at that hour."

99

Davidson, normally an astonishingly facile sculptor, found he could not proceed. At his studio, he stared at the photograph of the painting of the President. Davidson did not like it. It was another artist's interpretation, not his. "The President did not look that way to me," he later wrote. "Besides it was ridiculous to do a bas-relief from a photograph when you could do it from life." Four days went by, and Davidson had nothing to show for it. "I was getting nowhere," he wrote.

Believing that he could presume on his friendship with the President, he telephoned the White House and asked for a sitting. It was December 30. "The President agreed to sit for me," he recalled. "I flew to Washington and the President posed for me that same afternoon. He was most sympathetic with my plight and offered to give me another sitting the following afternoon."

Davidson worked with great intensity, as he normally did. He modelled the portrait in wax. He felt, as he recalled later, that he had to work desperately to make up for the time lost, and he had no time for socializing, even when one of Roosevelt's White House lieutenants, Stephen Early, came into the oval office with a bottle of brandy and three glasses. *He offered one to the President, handed me mine and proposed a toast,* Davidson recalled. *I raised my glass, gulped it down, and went on working. Steve Early was horrified and said to the President, "Look at that Frenchman." I was too busy to sip the brandy in the traditional French manner.*

Now that he was no longer trying to copy another's work, now that he had his own chance to portray the President, Davidson had come up with an innovative idea for the style of the medal. He discussed it with Roosevelt. He had seen and admired an ancient coin, struck in gold at Syracuse. The rough-hewn coin had a dignity, even a nobility, to it that had caught Davidson's fancy. He wanted that antique Greek coin to influence the medal he was now making. He proposed modelling the portrait in a somewhat primitive, rough style, if Roosevelt approved. Roosevelt enthusiastically endorsed the idea: the inaugural medal would suggest the glories of Greek art in the Golden Age. Thus encouraged, Davidson bent to his labor.

Working in the White House, he had the portrait completed on time, on December 31, New Year's Eve. Meanwhile, the Mint's engraver, Sinnock, had finished his model for the reverse. He had sketched at least two preliminary designs before deciding on the one submitted. Not surprisingly, he designed a conventional, modern reverse, in jarring contrast to the portrait submitted by Davidson. Obviously, in the rush to complete their work, Davidson and Sinnock had not consulted adequately with each other. Sinnock had made no effort to bring his reverse into harmony with the Davidson portrait. He had used the traditional motif of oak leaves and laurel—the oak leaves to suggest strength and courage, the laurel an award of honor—about the inaugural date. Davidson had used a rough technique, the circle about the portrait irregular and uncertain, in the manner of the coin from ancient Syracuse. Sinnock's reverse was geometrically perfect. The conflict was a matter of considerable concern to Mrs. Ross.

Working at breakneck pace, the Mint's workers produced the first replica of the medal on January 13, a week before inauguration day, and it was rushed to Mrs. Ross in Washington, who sent it to President Roosevelt for his approval. She herself was troubled by the Davidson portrait. The artist had obviously not prepared her for his rough-hewn design, nor told her that the President had approved the concept. *The fact is that when the inaugural medal first arrived in the Bureau for our inspection,* she wrote at the time, *all of us [were] somewhat startled at the roughness of the finish. The irregular, hoop-like circle around the portrait troubled me; I even sent word, when it was submitted to the President, that the circle could be straightened out if he desired. The word came back to me that by no means would he have it done; that he wanted the whole thing left just as it was; that it was suggestive of an old Greek coin.*

President Roosevelt took special delight in Mrs. Ross's misunderstanding of what Davidson had attempted, and he told Chairman Davies with relish just what the artist had in mind and how the Mint officials had misinterpreted it. Davies knew that Davidson would enjoy Roosevelt's remarks and he wrote him what the President had said: *He told me of the interesting conversation he had with you in which you suggested that you wished to work out a coin which would have some distinctive form and that you mentioned that the design be after the manner of some ancient coin of Syracuse upon which was the head of one of the rulers of the day, executed in a rough surface impressed into the metal and surrounded by an edge varied in regularity.*

He got quite a chuckle out of it when he told me that one of the inaugural officials had been very much disturbed over this very feature that you had executed in the inaugural medal, being concerned lest the President not be pleased with it.

The President expressed himself in terms of great admiration of your genius.

On January 14, as soon as she received word from the White House, Mrs. Ross telegraphed to the Superintendent of the Mint at Philadelphia that the President had approved the sample medal "unconditionally." She authorized the Mint to proceed immediately with the thousand replicas in bronze. The committee authorized only one in gold, and this was presented to President Roosevelt by Mrs. Ross and other members of her committee on January 29 at the White House. The President told Mrs. Ross he would place the medal in a private collection for his children. The committee also authorized the Mint to strike two of the medals in silver, one for Chairman Davies, the other for Mrs. Ross.

Ambassador Davies liked the Davidson medal so much that he later had several mounted in silver ashtrays which he gave to White House staffers and personal friends.

Under the contract, the Mint charged the Inaugural Committee 50 cents for each bronze medal struck, or $500 for the total number ordered, plus $15 for boxes, and $115 for the dies. Roosevelt's gold medal cost $90.45, and the silver medals $5.85 each.

The committee put the inaugural medals on sale in Washington on January 16, four days before the inauguration. They were quickly sold out, to the surprise of the members of the medals committee. This was so for several reasons. The price, as President Roosevelt had suggested it should be, was low. The sculptor was one of

Roosevelt inaugural medal
Jo Davidson and John Sinnock
Gold, 42 mm
Franklin D. Roosevelt Library and Museum

the foremost artists of his time. The occasion for striking these medals, a third presidential inauguration, was unique. The committee had suggested in its advertising that the medal would almost certainly increase in value in the years ahead.

Mrs. Ross immediately reported to officials of the Inaugural Committee that all the medals had been sold, and she asked permission to strike another thousand replicas. There was no time to call a meeting of the full executive committee of the Inaugural Committee. Alfons B. Landa, executive assistant to Inaugural Chairman Davies, after consulting other officials, authorized the Mint to strike the additional medals. He suggested, however, that the second run should carry a diminutive "2" inconspicuously on the medal's reverse, to differentiate this issue from the first. Mrs. Ross so instructed the officials at the Mint, and thus a die variety was created. These medals also sold quickly, and a few days after the inauguration, the medals committee authorized still another thousand medals to meet orders already received. These also carried the "2" on the reverse.

The Inaugural Committee quickly sold the thousand medals originally struck, and ordered another two thousand. These second-edition medals were marked on the reverse with a "2." Private collection

Despite the uniqueness of the occasion, the first third-term inauguration, the 1941 Inaugural Committee lost money. Again there had been no official ball, traditionally a chief fund-raiser, and the committee also lost money on the grandstands built for the parade. It did make a profit on the inaugural gala and on the official inaugural program, but not enough to offset the other losses. Local firms and citizens had contributed $130,414 to the traditional Guarantee Fund, and these contributors suffered the losses, receiving back only $120,146.34.

The medals committee, however, showed a modest profit. Sales totalled $2,970.34, and the expenses ran to $2,093.65, not counting the cost of the dies or the gold medal for President Roosevelt. The medal had paid for itself.

President Roosevelt was especially pleased with Davidson's portrait. It brought favorable comment from many quarters, and indeed proved so successful that officials at the Mint briefly considered using it for a larger medal in its regular series of presidential medals. On his part, Roosevelt not only invited Davidson to attend the inauguration, but he also invited him to lunch at the White House "immediately after the inaugural ceremonies at the Capitol."

On the President's birthday, ten days later, Davidson sent him a telegram: "I celebrate this day." Roosevelt wrote him a thank-you note, and at the bottom of it he scribbled another message: "The medal is grand—the Oligarch of ancient Syracuse approves."

The Inaugural Committee
requests the honor of the presence of

Honorable and Mrs. Henry Agard Wallace

to attend and participate in the Inauguration of

Franklin Delano Roosevelt

as President of the United States of America

and

Henry Agard Wallace

as Vice President of the United States of America
on Monday the twentieth of January
one thousand nine hundred and forty-one
in the City of Washington

Please reply to
The Inaugural Committee
District Building
Washington, D. C.

Joseph E. Davies
Chairman

*Henry Wallace's invitation to his own inauguration as Vice President. Roosevelt wrote,
on his invitation, "I'll go if I can find the time."*
Private collection

FDR	1941	1	gold	(42 mm)	1
FDR	1941	2	silver	(42 mm)	2
FDR	1941	3	bronze (type 1)	(42 mm)	1,000
FDR	1941	4	bronze (type 2)	(42 mm)	2,000

FRANKLIN D. ROOSEVELT
1945

In November 1944, President Roosevelt won reelection to a fourth term. The country was engaged in a world war, with momentous military operations in Europe and the Pacific. Franklin Roosevelt wanted the inaugural ceremony to be spare, austere, and dignified. There was no need to create the usual Inaugural Committee to conduct the traditional "unofficial" celebrations.

All the same, the presentation of a gold medal to the President had become a tradition unbroken since the second inauguration of William McKinley in 1901. Nellie Tayloe Ross, Director of the United States Mint, knew this and it worried her. The Mint doubtlessly would be expected to produce that inaugural medal. In late November, she telephoned Senator Robert Flood Byrd of Virginia and asked for help. He was chairman of the joint congressional Inaugural Committee in charge of the swearing-in ceremony.

Byrd's committee considered the matter. The congressional Inaugural Committee had never had anything to do with medals. That was the traditional responsibility of the citizens' committee that conducted the "unofficial" celebration. Mrs. Ross was so informed.

The message obviously gave her little help. There were valid reasons why no inaugural medal should be struck this year. Copper and bronze were in short supply because of war demands. The Mint was engaged in war production of its own, with no spare time or energy for such frivolities as inaugural medals. "It is probable," she wrote in early December, "that in due time the President and the Secretary of the Treasury will realize that there is no medal in prospect and will call on the Mint to produce one." As Director of the Mint, she did not want to be caught short. She wrote to her departmental superior, Undersecretary of the Treasury Daniel W. Bell, requesting help. She told Bell that, in 1941, the Mint had made the inaugural medal for Roosevelt and had to work under intense pressure because the decision had come so late. "The sculptor had to go to the White House at night, New Year's Eve, to model the President's head," she wrote. "Mint people at Philadelphia had to take long drives at night in private cars to the sculptor's country home for conferences." It took time to make a model, more time to cut the dies, still more time to strike the medals. There were other problems: who would authorize the operation and take responsibility for the expense of production and distribution? Always before, she wrote Bell, these responsibilities had been assumed by the citizens' Inaugural Committee. She suggested that Bell call the matter to the attention of the Secretary of the Treasury, Henry Morgenthau, Jr., because he probably would wish to bring it to the attention of the President. "Art," she wrote, "is something which, as you know, cannot be satisfactorily evolved in a hurry."

Mrs. Ross had a short-cut in mind to get a new medal in the Mint's presses as quickly as possible. "If it were acceptable to the President to have the Jo Davidson portrait of four years ago, again used, changing the reverse," she wrote, "the problem of design would be solved." A Mint engraver could quickly produce a new reverse.

Undersecretary Bell acted promptly, and so, apparently, did Bell's boss, Secretary Morgenthau. By December 12, Bell had relayed to Mrs. Ross that the President did want another inaugural medal.

On the 12th, Mrs. Ross telephoned Jo Davidson. She told him she was merely sounding him out, asking for his advice concerning a new medal. *He exclaimed at once that he understood perfectly,* she wrote to Bell, *that he wanted very much to make the design himself; that he was not greatly concerned about being paid, that he knew the kind of design he wanted to make, said it would be entirely different in type from the last one and would show the other side of the President's face. I gathered that he would not reject pay for his work, but would, in any case, expect his expenses to be paid. He said he would go anywhere to the President to model his head and would do so right away.*

President Roosevelt had left Washington at the end of November for a rest at his favorite vacation place, Warm Springs, Georgia. He returned to Washington on December 20, and two days later a group designated "The Inaugural Planning Committee" met at the White House. In the group was Joseph E. Davies, chairman of the 1941 Inaugural Committee.

There were ticklish questions about inaugurating the President in the midst of a world war. His safety, of course, was a major concern. The group decided to hold the ceremony at the White House with relatively few persons invited. There would be a religious service beforehand at St. John's Episcopal Church across Lafayette Park from the White House. The President and his wife would host a modest buffet lunch at the White House immediately afterwards, and later that afternoon they would hold a tea. That was all.

As for the inaugural medal, President Roosevelt discussed it with Ambassador Davies. Could Davies take on the responsibility? He would, of course. It was more involved than it sounded. Normally, the Inaugural Committee financed its medals committee, allowing advance funds to pay bills as they were due. The medals committee later would repay that advance from sales. There were no such funds available now and no staff to handle the details without prior payment. Davies resolved all these problems at once. He agreed himself to pay for all the medals, and he offered his private office staff to handle the distribution. He would be reimbursed as the medals were sold.

"I regard you a committee of one appointed by President Roosevelt to determine all matters relating to that medal," Mrs. Ross wrote to him. It was true. There could have been no inaugural medal in 1945 if someone had not stepped forward to assume the financial responsibility.

Davies asked Mrs. Ross and two of his colleagues, Melvin Hildreth and Alfons Landa, to join him as members of this inaugural medals committee. All of them had served on the 1941 Inaugural Committee. They had no problem asking Jo Davidson to sculpt the inaugural medal.

Roosevelt readily agreed to sit for Davidson, and the sculptor came to the White House in late December to model the President again from life. "Those were busy days for him," Davidson later wrote in his memoirs, "and I had to wait around while he found a few precious minutes for me." Davidson took full advantage of his opportunities. He modelled an extraordinarily sensitive portrait, in right profile. To suggest the President's wartime role as Commander-in-Chief, Davidson cloaked him in a Navy cape. Roosevelt had always regarded himself as a naval man. *While I was working on his profile,* Davidson wrote, *he suggested that the reverse of the medal should*

Roosevelt inaugural medal
Jo Davidson
Gold, 45 mm
Franklin D. Roosevelt Library
and Museum

carry the U.S.S. Constitution *in full sail, with the inscription, "Thou too sail on, O Ship of State, Sail on O Union strong and great." The President had a painting of the* Constitution *which he had brought down and sent to the Willard Hotel, where I sat up all night working on it.*

While I was working on the portrait for the medal in the White House office, the President picked up a beautifully bound Christmas book and inscribed it "To Jo Davidson in search of light." This was in reference to my shifting from place to place in order to see him better. But it carried a deeper meaning for me.

President Roosevelt had made the same request to Paul Manship in 1932. Thus Davidson duplicated Manship's theme, but his treatment of it was strikingly different. Manship's reverse spoke symbolically; Davidson's design carried the plastic naturalism so long his great strength. As before, he worked in wax, and he kept his model to the same seven-inch diameter he had used in 1941, again, presumably, to save time preparing the dies.

Meanwhile, Davies and Mrs. Ross settled negotiations with the Mint. They decided on a medal one-and-three-quarters inches in diameter, slightly larger than the 1941 medal. That meant a higher price, $2.00 each. They also decided to produce the same number—three thousand—as four years before. The Mint agreed to strike these medals for 80 cents apiece, plus the cost of making the dies, another $300.

Davidson turned in his models as soon as he had them completed. He did not take time to letter in the chosen words; that was done by the Mint's engravers. Mrs. Ross was delighted with Davidson's work. She wrote to him on January 5: "If you could hear, in the conference concerning the medal, the applause of the fine spirit in which you have taken over this project, it would, I think, give you satisfaction." "I feel," Davidson replied, "that my labors have not been in vain, and it is a very satisfactory feeling."

On January 9, Mrs. Ross received a trial strike of the new medal, the first made. She wrote promptly to congratulate the artist: "It is a splendid product of your skill. The character you have put in the President's face is remarkable; the likeness is excellent too. The ship on the reverse is beautiful, making altogether a gem of a medal."

On January 12, the first bronze medal arrived in Washington, and Ambassador Davies called the few members of his ad hoc medals committee into session at the White House to look at it. Then he dispatched it by White House mail pouch to the President, who was at his home in Hyde Park, New York. "Your hard working (?)

Medals Committee, here in session," Davies wrote to him, "have just received the first inaugural medal struck off by the Mint. We hasten to forward it to you." Roosevelt had asked about the medal the day before, and Davies wished no delay in getting it to him. He also told the President that the medals ordered would be in Washington in time for the inauguration and that he understood the President had approved the design. If he had not done so, Davies added, it was too late now to make any changes.

As pledged, the Mint had the medals in Washington in time, two thousand on January 18 and the other thousand the next day. To meet demand, Davies later approved another five hundred.

On January 18, Roosevelt had returned to Washington, and Davies and his three committee members, along with Jo Davidson, presented him with the gold inaugural medal. Waiting to see the President that day, in the White House office of his military aide, General Edwin "Pa" Watson, they feared that Davidson's portrait made the President look too old, too ill. "When, a moment later, we entered the President's office and looked into his face," wrote Mrs. Ross, "all of us, I think, recognized with a pang the ravages that illness and the strain of work and worry had wrought."

Jo Davidson presenting the gold medal to President Roosevelt. Standing, left to right, are members of the medals committee: Joseph Davies, chairman; Melvin Hildreth; and Alfons Landa. Photograph courtesy Mrs. Lowell Russell Ditzen

Roosevelt was in a gay mood, all the same. When Davidson handed him the gold medal, he burst into laughter. "Jo," he said, "this is all wrong. I never wear a bow tie with a Navy cape!" The sculptor was not the least rattled. "You wore a bow tie, Mr. President," he replied, "when you posed for this." Everyone laughed.

The President was to leave shortly after the inauguration for a summit conference at Yalta. After that, he planned to sail to the Middle East, there to confer with the Arab leaders. Remembering this now, Roosevelt turned to "Pa" Watson. "What does Ibn Saud want for a present?" he asked, about the King of Saudi Arabia.

Watson replied that the King had indicated privately that he would like one of America's latest passenger airplanes, the DC-3.

"How much would that cost?" Roosevelt asked Watson.

Even in its military version, this airplane would cost many thousands of dollars. The President would have to give the King an especially appointed version. Watson made an estimate of that cost.

The President then turned to Mrs. Ross and asked her the cost of the gold medal he had just received. That was $125. He thought a moment. Then he turned to Watson again. "Let's give the King one of these gold medals of me," the President said. He thought a moment longer, and then added, "I might just as well give old Joe one."

In the end, Roosevelt asked for five inaugural medals in gold. The Mint obviously had to rush to prepare them. At the Livadia Palace at Yalta, on February 10, he gave these gold medals to Joseph Stalin and Winston Churchill, and also to their respective foreign ministers, V. M. Molotov and Anthony Eden. Three days later, at Great Bitter Lake, Egypt, aboard the U.S.S. *Quincy*, Roosevelt met with King Ibn Saud. He gave him the fifth gold inaugural medal. By then, he had thought better about ignoring the King's expressed desires for a DC-3, and made that a present also.

Later, the committee members authorized special inaugural medals for themselves. Ambassador Davies and Mrs. Ross received gold medals, and Hildreth and Landa received silver. They each paid for them.

After Roosevelt's death in April, Ambassador Davies had the mint prepare a gold-plated galvano of the Davidson portrait, and he presented it to the Roosevelt Library at Hyde Park. Subsequently, the committee had the Mint strike a pair of the gold medals and presented them also to the Roosevelt Library. Mounted in a special case, these two medals were delivered in July 1946.

FDR	1945	1	gold	(45 mm)	10
FDR	1945	2	silver	(45 mm)	2
FDR	1945	3	bronze	(45 mm)	3,500

HARRY S
TRUMAN
1949

Almost no one expected Harry S Truman to win the 1948 presidential election, and his unexpected, stunning victory guaranteed that his inauguration would be an exuberant one. The Inaugural Committee of private citizens came quickly into being; Melvin Hildreth, who had served on all Franklin Roosevelt's Inaugural Committees, was named Chairman. In 1945, he had been one of the three members of Ambassador Davies's truncated committee to commission that year's inaugural medal. With Truman's permission, the Inaugural Committee planned an extravagant, joyous celebration, complete with a ball, a gala, and a full-scale parade. To meet initial costs, committee members sought to amass the largest Guarantee Fund in history; they planned an inauguration on the largest scale ever.

Hildreth appointed Nellie Tayloe Ross as chairman of the medals committee. Still Director of the United States Mint, Mrs. Ross knew fully the difficulties of creating and producing a medal in time for the inauguration. She acted quickly. On November 16, she appointed four members to her committee, and she wrote to Chairman Hildreth requesting full authority to engage "a sculptor of recognized standing" to design the inaugural medal. "I have in mind C. P. Jennewein of New York," she wrote, "who, I am confident, has no superiors." Long used to her own authority, Mrs. Ross did not wait for even the first meeting of her committee to commission Jennewein (1890—). She telephoned him, as soon as she received clearance from Hildreth to commit the funds—$1,000—for the medal design. She assumed, and so did everyone else apparently, that the Mint would strike the medal. It had been doing so since 1929, with only the 1937 medal excepted.

She had pronounced ideas on just how the medal should be made, and what should be done with it. "It is my idea," she wrote on November 22, "that it should be made a source of profit to the Committee." For two decades, the medals committees had been satisfied to make enough money from the sales to pay for production. Mrs. Ross wanted publicity for this new medal, and she wanted the Inaugural Committee to sell as many of them as possible. Their sales could help defray the cost of the entire inauguration, a far cry from the years when the medal had been an out-of-pocket cost to the committee.

Mrs. Ross again talked to the sculptor by telephone. She urged swiftness on him. The committee would like the designs for the obverse and reverse within two weeks, if possible, or no later than three weeks. She wanted Jennewein to work from photographs in modelling the President's portrait, and she arranged to send him such photographs as were available. Surprisingly, the White House had only two.

On November 23, she wrote to Jennewein, cautioning him about the relief of his design: "It should be, of course, high enough to be impressive in effect," she wrote. "We would not want it flat like a coin and yet if it were excessively high it might require an undue number of strikes to produce. I am sure that your judgment will be good on that point." This was the traditional worry of the minters, and their perpetual quarrel with the sculptors. The mint masters worried about cost: every strike on the medal's planchet added to it. The sculptors worried about artistic merit: normally the bolder the relief, the better, as far as they were concerned. Jennewein was later to resent that Chairman Ross and the Mint lowered his relief on the Truman portrait.

Mrs. Ross also asked Jennewein to consider carefully the wording of the inscriptions and to submit his ideas to her committee before proceeding with an actual model. To help Jennewein, she telephoned Gilroy Roberts, the Mint's chief sculptor, in Philadelphia, and asked him to strike off on cardboard, or some similar material, replicas of the previous inaugural medals for Jennewein's examination. With appropriate discretion, she added the instruction that these sample strikes were to be returned to the Mint and destroyed after Jennewein had seen them.

Assuring Jennewein that "your own ideas, needless to say, are to control," Mrs. Ross nevertheless suggested that it might be undesirable to use an eagle on the reverse of the medal: "Because of its constant appearance on Government documents and works of every kind something more unusual would be pleasing." By then Jennewein had already designed a rough sketch for the reverse, which he sent to her on November 24. *As you will note,* he wrote in the accompanying letter, *I am using a wreath of alternating Laurel and Oak, as a symbol of Strength and Glory. This will connect the symbolism with the Seal of the United States where I have the cloud-burst (which is above the Eagle's head) with the thirteen stars and below the escutcheon.* Mrs. Ross did not like it. In all, Jennewein sketched at least nine different designs for the reverse, trying to meet her criteria, and in the end he was exasperated with her demands. "She wanted to tell people she was responsible for the reverse," he said, years later. "She told that damned sculptor!" All the same, he did feel "the honor and the privilege," as he phrased it, of being commissioned to make such a medal for such an occasion.

*One of Jennewein's first sketches for
the reverse of the Truman inaugural medal
Private collection*

If Jennewein would take instruction on the design of the reverse of the medal, he bristled at the very thought of anyone interfering with his portrait of President Truman for the obverse. The portrait of the President would be Jennewein's alone! He would brook no interference there.

He had, in fact, exceptional skill in relief portraiture, and he was dissatisfied with the photographs of Truman which had been provided. He wanted his own. He telephoned a Washington photographer, and he asked Mrs. Ross to arrange an appointment. Almost immediately, he changed his mind. Photographs would not serve. He telephoned Mrs. Ross and asked her to see if she could make an appointment for him with the President. She said she would try to make the arrangements for the following week.

On November 24, Mrs. Ross met with her medals committee for the first time. She had on hand cost estimates from the Mint: the medal in the "usual" size would cost 95 cents. The committee therefore recommended that it be sold for $2.00 plus 15 cents for mailing charges, and that three thousand be struck initially.

As the minutes of this meeting show, the committee wanted publicity for their medal: "It is suggested that there probably is a wide market for the medals throughout the country, especially collectors, and that if adequate publicity is given and a good mail order system established, a large number could be disposed of."

The committee, for the first time ever, considered marketing silver replicas of the inaugural medal. The Mint had estimated that it could produce these for about $20 each, and the committee members believed they could sell them for as much as $30 each.

By December 6, Jennewein had in hand a drawing of what would prove to be the final design for the reverse: a woman wearing the Phrygian Cap, which symbolizes freedom, and holding a branch of laurel. "At her feet," he wrote to Mrs. Ross, "is a group representing the people of the nation whose privileges and civil rights she is guarding."

Two days later, Jennewein received a telephone call. He had his appointment with President Truman: at the White House the next morning, December 9, at 8:30. Mrs. Ross had made the arrangements. The sculptor had already roughed out a model of Truman in Plasticine, and he took this with him that afternoon when he flew to Washington. He checked into the Hotel Washington, two blocks from the White House.

The design for the reverse went through
many stages before Jennewein arrived at the final version.
Private collection

As by arrangement, Jennewein met with the President's secretary, Matthew Connally, the next morning and was escorted into the Oval Office. After brief introductions, he went to work. So did Truman, ignoring him. Jennewein sat on a corner of the President's desk, while the President swiftly went through a two-foot stack of mail with Connally taking dictation. The light was poor for Jennewein's purpose, and he was somewhat awed at working in the Oval Office, but not so awed that he was not shocked to see the President "wasting his time answering his mail." Jennewein also was startled at the way President Truman made federal appointments, one of his chores that morning. "They were handling appointments like groceries," he said later.

Jennewein struggled to capture Truman's likeness in the clay. He was not happy with his model. "Mr. Truman," he said, "I haven't got you yet and I've sat here two hours. Would you mind stepping out in the hall?" He had seen that the hallway had a full window and offered far better light than the President's office.

Truman had no objections at all. "Why, sure, sculptor," he said. "I've only got ten minutes. I've got the press coming in." In the bright, full light of the hallway, Jennewein was surprised at Truman's extraordinarily healthy complexion. "What a handsome beautiful complexion!" he exclaimed. "Well," the President said, with a laugh, "that's why I take my walks."

Jennewein was delighted with the new arrangement. The light was perfect. "He stood there like a soldier," Jennewein said later. "In that ten minutes I did more work than I did in the previous two hours."

Jennewein liked what he had now. He felt he had captured the President just the way he wanted him. He had had no advance notions about what he wanted to express in Truman's portrait. "Just do it!" he had told himself. He had no thought of not using the President's eyeglasses. "He couldn't see a damn thing without his glasses," he explained.

Truman rushed off to meet the press corps, and Jennewein was annoyed. The President had never looked at his portrait. "That embarrassed me a little bit," the sculptor said. "I usually find that fellows like to see what they look like in the model. If I was doing your portrait, you'd look over my shoulder and take a look. He didn't."

The medals committee met on December 15 and approved Jennewein's model. At the same time, the committee decided to make this inaugural medal slightly larger than the one for President Roosevelt in 1945. The Truman medal would be two inches in diameter. The committee asked Jennewein to add his name to the medal and the appropriate Latin phrase *F Ad Vivum,* to show that he had modelled the President from life.

On December 20, the medals committee gave its approval to the reverse which Jennewein had fashioned to Mrs. Ross's desires. By then, he had changed his own sense of the symbolic meaning of his model: "The figure symbolizes Liberty with a laurel Branch in her hand, denoting preeminence. The massed figures below, looking up, suggest the aspirations of humanity for Freedom."

The committee members deliberately sought publicity for this inaugural medal. They issued a formal press release and asked radio stations around the country to broadcast an announcement about the medal, telling how it could be purchased. The committee imposed only one restriction: all orders had to be received by January 22, 1949.

The medals sold quickly. Orders for three thousand were on hand by January 13. The day before, Mrs. Ross had ordered another thousand medals in bronze. By the deadline, the committee had ordered and sold 7,500 inaugural medals—the largest number ever sold or struck for one inauguration.

On January 14, the medals committee met President Truman at the White House, and Mrs. Ross presented him with the inaugural medal struck in gold. "The

Galvano for the Truman inaugural medal, 245 mm
Private collection

President seemed to be very pleased with the medal," the committee's minutes read, "and expressed his appreciation."

The committee members also had the Mint strike a gold replica for Melvin Hildreth, Chairman of the Inaugural Committee, and another in gold for Mrs. Ross. They abandoned the idea of selling the inaugural medal in silver, but they granted permission to strike nine of the Truman medals in silver. Two of these were awarded to Washington companies for their inauguration displays. The others went to members of the Inaugural Committee.

Not surprisingly, Truman's inauguration proved a financial success. The ball, the parade, and the gala all returned a profit which repaid in full the Guarantee Fund of $258,405 and still left an additional $54,947 for distribution to local charities.

Truman inaugural medal
Carl Paul Jennewein
Silver, 51 mm
Private collection

Significantly, the inaugural medals committee also showed a profit. It spent $10,834.96 on producing and distributing the medals, and it received gross returns of $14,986.75. The Mint, as with the previous inaugural medals, charged the Inaugural Committee the mere cost of production. The 1949 inaugural medals committee had, for the first time, shown that the medals could be sold on a national scale and at a profit. That was something for the next Inaugural Committee to remember and something for a private mint, perhaps, to notice.

HST	1949	1	gold	(51 mm)	3
HST	1949	2	silver	(51 mm)	9
HST	1949	3	bronze	(51 mm)	7,500

DWIGHT D. EISENHOWER
1953

In 1952, for the first time in twenty years, the Republicans won the White House. Dwight David Eisenhower was elected by a landslide. For Republicans, this would be a time of special rejoicing, and they wanted the inauguration to symbolize, as well as to initiate, the change. The Inaugural Committee, quickly appointed, planned a massive, spectacular celebration. They collected more than $680,000 for the Guarantee Fund, and scheduled two inaugural balls, among other festivities. Eisenhower's political advisers picked Joseph C. McGarraghy, a prominent Washington attorney active in local politics, as Chairman of the Inaugural Committee. Significantly, McGarraghy and those immediately associated with him had a special desire to encourage private enterprise in any way they could.

Nellie Tayloe Ross, a Democrat, still held the post of Director of the United States Mint. She assumed that the Mint again would strike the inaugural medal, and accordingly she made preparations at the Mint to do just that. Her plans, however, were unexpectedly challenged. Clyde C. Trees, president of the Medallic Art Company, decided to try to persuade this "private enterprise" administration coming to power to award the contract to his New York firm. He called on officials of the Inaugural Committee to make his case. They were indeed interested, and Chairman McGarraghy needed no persuasion. It was his own bent. "I took the view," he said years later, "that with Ike coming in as President, it was a good idea to promote the idea of free enterprise." In any event, Trees was encouraged to bid for the medal contract, and he did so. Medallic Art suggested it be two-and-three-quarters inches in diameter, and Trees offered to make these in bronze for $1.10 each on a large order.

Before the Medallic Art Company offered its bid, Chairman McGarraghy had appointed two inaugural medals committees—one under the chairmanship of Mrs L. Corrin Strong to handle design and contract, and the other under the chairmanship of Gilbert Hahn, Jr., to handle sales and distribution. Mrs. Strong's committee selected Walker Hancock (1901—), a distinguished sculptor, to design the Eisenhower medal.

On November 28, 1952, Mrs. Strong's committee chose the Medallic Art Company to produce the medal. In announcing the decision, Mrs. Strong stated that price and time, not political philosophy, had decided the case against the United States Mint. She said that both the Mint and the Medallic Art Company had offered to make the medals at "cost," but that the private firm's estimates were below those of the Mint by a "considerable" amount. She also said that the Mint could not assure delivery in the quantity needed before inauguration day, unless the sculptor, Walker Hancock, could deliver his finished models by December 8. The private company, under its proposal, could allow Hancock until December 25, Christmas Day.

Actually, Mrs. Strong's analysis of the terms misread the proposals of the two bidders. A charge at "cost," for the Mint, included considerable overhead and overtime charges not required by a private firm. Moreover, although the Medallic Art

Company did underbid the Mint, its proposal was not to produce the medals at cost, but, in the spirit of free enterprise, at a profit.

The decision to award the contract to a private firm was one of the most important moments in the history of inaugural medals, as significant as the decision in 1929 to sell rather than give them to the inauguration workers. The 1929 decision had kept alive the tradition of these medals. The 1953 decision led to their mass production and made them a major financial consideration for every future Inaugural Committee.

Walker Hancock, meanwhile, had met with President-elect Eisenhower at his headquarters at the Hotel Commodore in New York City. Eisenhower had agreed to pose for him, but he found little time to do so, except between appointments.

At their first meeting, Hancock said that he wanted to portray him in full profile. Eisenhower objected. "They've done me in profile before," he explained, "not successfully." He asked Hancock to model him in three-quarters profile. Hancock assented, and made the attempt, but he did not like the result. Neither did Eisenhower, who then agreed to a portrait in full profile.

The sculptor had a continuing problem. In repose, the general's face turned somber, his expression grim. "I didn't want to put that on the medal," Hancock said later. He wanted a more cheerful portrait. He tried to draw Eisenhower out of his grave mood.

"I have a message for you that I'm a little embarrassed to deliver to you," he told Eisenhower. "It's from a young lady who sends you her love."

Eisenhower wheeled on Hancock, as though angry.

"It's from my five-year-old daughter," Hancock said.

Eisenhower burst out laughing. "Isn't that a wonderful age?" he said to the sculptor. "I have a five-year-old grandson."

"That," said Hancock later, "broke the ice. From then on, he was a changed person." Eisenhower's face became animated and alive, no longer somber and grim. Hancock took advantage of the change, working quickly to capture the more cheerful expression. Even so, the pose was more serious than Eisenhower himself liked. He examined Hancock's finished portrait, and said, "You've done mighty well by me, but if you'll just turn the lip of my mouth up." Hancock made the change.

For the reverse of the medal, Hancock had difficulty deciding on a design. He made a few sketches, two of them showing clasped hands. These were rejected by Mrs. Strong's design committee. Instead, the committee proposed an eagle and some reference to Eisenhower's career. A suggestion was made that Hancock use the presidential seal, but Eisenhower rejected that idea. "Will this medal be available before the inauguration?" Eisenhower asked. "Yes," replied Hancock, "about four days before." Eisenhower did not believe the seal should be used until he was President.

Hancock asked Eisenhower to suggest ideas for the reverse.

"Well, now," Eisenhower answered, "what shall it be? Our armed forces? No. Friendship with our neighbors? That's difficult, isn't it?" He thought for a moment. He did not want any laudatory reference to himself. He wanted simplicity. "I'm from the West," he said, "but we don't have covered wagons anymore."

"No," said Hancock, "but your state grows more wheat than any other state. We might use that."

"That's a good idea," Eisenhower said. "We'll use that."

Hancock designed a wheat border for the reverse, surrounding a symbolic eagle and an inscription. The eagle clasped an olive branch in its right talons, a group of arrows in its left. "The wings of the eagle are spread," the committee stated, in describing the medal, "and its head is turned in the same direction as the talon holding the olive branch, symbolizing the nation's prayers for lasting peace." This was no idle matter, symbolically. The United States had been for more than two years deeply engaged in war in Korea, and there was a tradition that the direction of the eagle's head—whether toward the olive branch or the warlike arrows—suggested the direction the incoming administration would take.

Hancock felt harried by the tremendous pressure on him to complete the models quickly. "A good medal," he said, "should take a couple of months of steady work." He had spent eleven days. The private mint reduced the relief on Hancock's portrait of the new President so that the medal could be finished with only four blows by the powerful presses. The sculptor was not upset. "The higher the relief, the better the medal," he stated, as the rule of thumb for sculptors. "You like a higher relief, but there are practical reasons for low relief."

Shortly after it had hardened the dies for Hancock's medal, the Medallic Art Company struck off some samples in silver. These were sent to Chairman McGarraghy and other officials of the Inaugural Committee. The company wanted the committee to authorize the sale of silver inaugural medals as well as bronze. No silver medals had ever before been sold to the public although, in 1949, the medals committee briefly considered this idea. "The market will probably be small," the 1949 committee had believed, according to its minutes, "but if authority is given, the number could be limited to those actually ordered and paid for in advance." The 1953 committee decided to make the experiment, on a small scale, and authorized the striking of a hundred medals in silver. Quickly, the members found that this was an inadequate number, and they increased the order to six hundred. Still later, they had to increase it again. A distributor suggested that these silver medals be numbered as struck, and this was done. The effect, of course, was to make the earlier sample silver medals, which were not numbered, a major die variety. The Medallic Art Company's records do not reflect how many of these unnumbered medals were struck in silver, but probably there were no more than a couple of dozen.

Chairman Hahn and his sales committee members undertook a spirited campaign to sell medals this year. They used the contacts of the Medallic Art Company to obtain free advertising in the numismatic and regular press. They set up booths at all the major functions of the inauguration, like the inaugural balls and the reception for state governors. "What we hoped," Hahn said later, "was that this would be such a unique and tangible thing from the inauguration that people would want them." He went to the public library in Washington and researched the background of these medals from old committee reports and other materials. He wrote a major article, the first in the field, on the tradition of inaugural medals. He took this article to the *Washington Evening Star,* the large afternoon newspaper in the capital, and asked that it be printed. Hahn concealed his own authorship, and the *Star* published it on January 19 as written by Joseph McGarraghy, Chairman of the Inaugural Committee. That, Hahn calculated, would give the article more impact on potential medal buyers.

Hahn also wrote a brochure on the Eisenhower medal for the Medallic Art Company. This gave a brief history of presidential inaugural medals and short biographies of President Eisenhower and the medal's sculptor, Walker Hancock. The company included it with each medal sold. Its purpose was to show the historic significance of these medals and thereby encourage further sales.

Hahn had still other ideas for selling the medals. He suggested, at one session of his committee, that the members put "the bite" on corporation chiefs to buy the medals in quantity as giveaways to their dealers and customers. "It seems to me," he wrote to Chairman McGarraghy, "that wider distribution could be had by sales through department stores, coin and stamp dealers, patriotic organizations, and Republican state organizations." Hahn himself wrote to all state Republican chairmen, urging them to encourage sales of the Eisenhower inaugural medal.

In all, the medal sales committee sold 788 medals in silver and 25,685 in bronze. The committee charged $24 each for the silver medals, which included the 20 percent federal excise tax, and $3.00 each for the bronze medals. Initially, Hahn had hoped to sell 10,000 medals, but his sales pitches had worked. The committee spent $49,176.43 in producing and marketing the medals, and it received total revenues of $86,235.17. That meant a profit of more than $37,000—far beyond expectations. Clearly, the inaugural medal had become important financially. The 1953 Inaugural Committee showed an excess of revenues over expenditures in the amount of $146,963, of which $130,000 was given to charities and the remainder reserved for the 1957 inauguration, another innovation. The silver medals alone returned more revenues—$16,696—than had all the 1949 medals, even though relatively few of them had been struck.

The Inaugural Committee authorized only one medal struck in gold in 1953, and this, of course, went to President Eisenhower. At the presentation, Clyde Trees of the Medallic Art Company told the President that his private firm had made the medal, and not the United States Mint as before. "This is a product of private enterprise," he said.

Eisenhower put his arm around Trees's shoulders, and said, "You're a man after my own heart."

Four years later, in 1957, the Medallic Art Company struck another 1953 Eisenhower inaugural medal in gold. This was done for Leonard Hall, then Repub-

Eisenhower inaugural medal
Walker Hancock
Gold, 70 mm
Mr. and Mrs. Leonard W. Hall

118

Eisenhower and other gold charms, replicas of the inaugural medals
The Honorable and Mrs. Gilbert Hahn, Jr.

lican National Chairman, who admired the 1957 inaugural gold medal he had received and asked for the 1953 medal also.

In 1953, the Medallic Art Company experimented with tiny replicas of the inaugural medal, and made dies of the obverse in four small sizes, the smallest approximately the size of a dime, the largest the size of a half-dollar. These were charms, potentially another field for exploitation. The company made a few of these gold charms for presentation to Mrs. Eisenhower, the wives of committee officials, and the sculptor's wife.

DDE	1953	1	gold	(70 mm)	2
DDE	1953	2	silver (unnumbered)	(70 mm)	25 (approx.)
DDE	1953	3	silver (serially numbered)	(70 mm)	788
DDE	1953	4	bronze	(70 mm)	25,685
DDE	1953	5	gold	(31 mm)	1
DDE	1953	6	gold	(21 mm)	18
DDE	1953	7	gold	(18 mm)	1

DWIGHT D. EISENHOWER
1957

President Eisenhower won overwhelming reelection in 1956, and the Inaugural Committee faced what traditionally had been a difficult assignment. A new President, taking the oath for the first time, normally has generated enormous enthusiasm among his supporters. His oath-taking has signalled a time of change, a new beginning for the American republic. The country and the world have hung on the words of his inaugural address, seeking to fathom the portents of his assuming charge of the executive branch of the government. All of this has created an excitement for the inauguration, and made easier the job of the Inaugural Committee: a high demand for tickets to the ball and the parade grandstands.

This has not been so for second inaugurations. By then, the country has known the President. His supporters have not felt the flush of victory; the reelection has marked only a continuation. Indeed, the President doubtlessly has campaigned for a second term on the plea that he be allowed to finish what he has started. The enthusiasm and the excitement surrounding the first inauguration long ago have been spent. All the same, the Inaugural Committee has to mount a full-scale celebration. To act otherwise would seem to be treating the President shabbily.

This was the situation in late 1956. A predicted shortage of funds and fears of flagging support put a special burden on the medals committees. Four years earlier, Gilbert Hahn and his sales committee had proved that the inaugural medal could be a solid money-raiser, and that its revenues could help defray the other inaugural costs. Hahn again had been named chairman of the medal sales committee. He knew from the start what was expected of him. "There was a lot of pressure," he said later, "to raise money." That, to Hahn, meant pressure to increase the sales and profits over 1953.

Within days after Eisenhower's reelection, Clyde C. Trees, chief officer of the Medallic Art Company, began an energetic campaign to win the contract for the 1957 inaugural medal. Leonard W. Hall, Republican National Chairman, appointed a Washington banker, Robert Fleming, as Chairman of the Inaugural Committee. This was the last time a national party chairman would do so. Under a new law passed by Congress in 1956, the President-elect hereafter would choose the inaugural chairman.

Trees wrote to Fleming and told him that the Medallic Art Company had made the first Eisenhower inaugural medal, and that the medal had proved such a success that the committee had sold more of them in 1953 than at all other inaugurations combined. "This," he wrote, "resulted in a substantial contribution towards the cost of the whole inaugural program."

Trees was obviously worried about the Mint winning the contract, and he took further steps to prevent that. Just a week after he wrote to Chairman Fleming, he sent another letter to Washington, this time to Senator Styles Bridges of New Hampshire, Chairman of the congressional Inaugural Committee, the group in charge of the ceremonies at the Capitol. He wanted Bridges to use his influence for the Medallic Art Company. "Our prices quoted on the last inaugural medals," Trees wrote to him, "were below the cost estimated by the Mint for reproducing the medals. We made a profit on the medal and delivered all of them well in advance of the earliest date the Mint could promise any." He thus argued that using his firm again would prove cheaper, faster, and more profitable to the Inaugural Committee. Trees's company did receive the contract, without any apparent competition from the Mint.

Meanwhile, committee officials had consulted Eisenhower about his medal. The President knew exactly what he wanted: the same sculptor who had designed his first medal, Walker Hancock. Further, Eisenhower told the committee officials that he would like the portrait of Vice President Richard Nixon on the medal with his own. The committee promptly notified Hancock that he had been selected, and Hancock as promptly informed the committee that he could not take the assignment. He had been named sculptor-in-residence of the American Academy in Rome. He was living there, and had heavy commitments to complete two major projects. He simply could not return to the United States at that time, even for the honor of designing the President's inaugural medal.

The medals committee could not accept Hancock's refusal. Eisenhower had asked for him. The committee informed him that he had received, in effect, a presidential command: he had to comply. They told Hancock that he could model the medal in Italy, and the committee and the medal company would arrange to fly the models to the United States. He did not need to return himself.

Hancock, of course, well knew Eisenhower's head. He had sculpted it with such skill that Eisenhower himself approved, although, as he had told Hancock in 1952, other sculptors who had tried had failed. Indeed, the President's face was still vivid in Hancock's memory. "I was immensely surprised by his face," he said of his sessions modelling Eisenhower, "by the angularity and squareness and ruggedness of it. I was really taken aback. Such a fine, angular head!" Moreover Hancock had his own model of Eisenhower's head. He repeated it in essential detail on the new medal. "I had to stick pretty close to the first head," he later explained.

Eisenhower–Nixon inaugural medal
Walker Hancock
Gold, 70 mm
Mr. and Mrs. Leonard W. Hall

121

The sculptor, however, did not like the requirement to include Nixon in the portrait. It made the design much more difficult to execute. "It's terribly hard to do a double portrait," he said. He worked from photographs to model the profile of Nixon, whom he had met. During one session in 1952, when Eisenhower was posing for him, Nixon walked into the room. Eisenhower introduced the two men. "We're discussing what should go on the reverse of the medal," Eisenhower said to Nixon. "Do you have any suggestions?" Nixon had none.

Hancock worked hurriedly on the new medal, and he concentrated on the portraits. "There was no chance," he said, "to make the reverse very interesting." He had no time. He contented himself by repeating the wreath of wheat shafts around the reverse, as in the 1953 medal, and then lettered in the full names of Eisenhower and Nixon. The wheat again symbolized the President's origins in Kansas.

Hancock had the models finished by the end of November and on their way, by air, to the Medallic Art Company in New York City. Concerned that the firm might lower the relief of his portraits too much, he wrote to the company on November 30 to caution them against doing so: "I hope that the relief will be kept as high as feasible. I *hate* low relief portraits on medals."

The firm acted quickly. Within a month, Hancock had received by air mail the first striking of the new Eisenhower inaugural medal. "The medal has just come— record time—and I am as delighted with the work as I am surprised by the speed with which it was done," he wrote to the firm. "The height of the relief is perfect."

Meanwhile, in Washington, Gilbert Hahn and his committee were trying to devise ways to sell more medals this year than in 1953. Hahn contacted Hancock, and asked him for any interesting information about the design that might help sales. "For my part," Hancock replied, "there is nothing to write about the medal this time, since I had no interview with the President and the design is so obvious that it must certainly speak for itself."

Hahn issued a press release announcing the new medals on December 13. He tried to make something of the double portraits, even though they were not unique. The medals on the badges of 1889, 1893, and 1897 had used portraits of both President and Vice President, and so had the inaugural medals of 1909 and 1937. *A good portion of the revenue to pay for the inaugural comes through the sale of these medals,* Hahn stated. *Since all inaugural costs with the exception of the Capitol swearing-in ceremonies must be paid for through the sale of tickets to the various events, or through the sale of official souvenirs, this is a very important item in the inaugural budget.*

In the contract with the Medallic Art Company, the price of the medals to the Inaugural Committee had been slightly increased from 1953. The bronze medals now cost the committee $1.27 each and the silver medals $10. The committee had initially ordered fifteen thousand of the medals in bronze, and five hundred in silver. For the bronze, the price was set at $3.50, and for the silver $27.50, both higher than four years before.

As before, the Medallic Art Company made special dies in three small sizes— ranging from a little less to a little more than an inch in diameter. The firm struck a few in gold, again for presentation to the First Lady and the wives of Inaugural Committee members. Hahn had toyed with the idea of trying to sell a charm-size medal as a souvenir. He thought that if they were struck in gold-filled metal, they might sell well at train stations, airports, and other public places. He discussed this with a jewelry firm in Rhode Island, on the chance that that company might offer better terms than the Medallic Art Company, and he also discussed, with officials of the inaugural ball committee, the idea of using such charms as favors at the ball.

Financially, the second inauguration of President Eisenhower proved a minor disaster. Those in charge of it consistently overestimated their revenues on every important item on their schedule, except the inaugural medals. Returns from the ball tickets, seats in the parade grandstands, and inauguration programs were disappointing. The committee officials blamed inclement weather for their financial failings, but the real cause was a lack of enthusiasm for the President's second inauguration. They had estimated overall revenues at $1,115,143, and they received actual revenues of only $889,116. The loss was borne by those who had contributed to the Guarantee Fund, who were repaid at the rate of $84.71 for every $100 contributed. The inauguration ceremonies took a total loss of $160,483.

Those losses would have been considerably higher except for the profits shown by the medals committee: 21,705 bronze medals sold and 1,033 silver medals. The sales netted a gross income of $94,885 against gross expenses of $47,653, for a net profit of $47,232. The 1957 medals committee made more money than the 1953 committee, with fewer sales, because of the higher prices charged.

The Inaugural Committee authorized gold inaugural medals for President Eisenhower and Vice President Nixon, and these were struck and presented. Leonard Hall, who had named Fleming chairman, liked this gold medal and he asked Fleming for one. This Fleming provided. Then, as mentioned in the previous chapter, Hall also asked him for the 1953 inaugural medal in gold. Fleming instructed the Medallic Art Company to make him one.

DDE	1957	1	gold	(70 mm)	3
DDE	1957	2	silver	(70 mm)	1,033
DDE	1957	3	bronze	(70 mm)	21,705
DDE	1957	4	gold	(30 mm)	2
DDE	1957	5	gold	(27 mm)	6
DDE	1957	6	gold	(21 mm)	4

JOHN F. KENNEDY
1961

The inaugural celebrations had become so complicated by 1957, with so little time from election day to inauguration day to organize the expected activities, that Robert V. Fleming, chairman of the 1957 Inaugural Committee, recommended that preparations for the next inauguration should begin well before election day on a bipartisan basis. Fleming's committee reserved some $20,000 for this purpose, and in July 1960, the Board of Commissioners of Washington, D.C., created the Pre-Inaugural Committee 1961, with the local Democratic and Republican party chairmen serving as co-chairmen. That committee created a nucleus staff for the regular Inaugural Committee, arranged for many necessary preparations, and suggested a preliminary budget. The group forecast overall expenditures of $703,000, of which $50,000 was suggested for production of inaugural medals to sell at an expected profit of $40,000. These estimates fell far short of the realities of the 1961 inauguration.

The Pre-Inaugural Committee urgently recommended that the President-elect designate the General Chairman of the Inaugural Committee as soon as possible after November 8, election day, "because of the serious time problem." John F. Kennedy, who became President-elect on that day, named Edward H. Foley, a prominent Washington lawyer, to the chairmanship. Foley, with the help of the advance work already done, promptly set about organizing the regular Inaugural Committee.

Unusually this year, Chairman Foley received an application for chairmanship of the medals committee. Bruce Sundlun, law partner of Gilbert Hahn, who had chaired the medals committee in 1953 and 1957, wrote to Foley just a week after Kennedy's election to volunteer for the post. Sundlun was a Democrat; his law partner was a Republican. From Hahn, Sundlun had learned a great deal about inaugural medals, and in his letter to Foley, he pointed out their financial significance, as well as the need to act promptly to have them ready by inauguration day.

The first decision was to choose a sculptor. The President-elect's wife, Jacqueline, was consulted, and she suggested Paul Manship, then the dean of American sculptors. In college, Mrs. Kennedy had written a term paper on Manship's work. Manship had made the inaugural medal for President Franklin Roosevelt in 1933. He was now almost seventy-five years old.

Meanwhile Sundlun, with another member of the medals committee, met with a representative of the Medallic Art Company, William Louth, and quickly came to an agreement. The company would produce the same-sized medals as in 1953 and 1957, at a charge of $10 for the silver and $1.35 for the bronze. These the committee would sell at $35 for the silver and $4.50 for the bronze. As an inducement to sales, the company suggested limiting the issue of silver medals to 7,500.

Sundlun proposed that the medals this year be sold through a national distributor. It was, he said later, "my only original idea." He negotiated a contract with the Coin & Currency Institute, under which the medals committee shared the royalties with the company, which, in turn, guaranteed to sell 6,500 of the silver medals and fifteen thousand of the bronze medals. That gave Sundlun a guaranteed profit of substantial proportions, and he informed Chairman Foley that the Inaugural Committee would receive at least $93,000, and possibly as much as $125,000, in profits from the inaugural medals.

Before the contract with Medallic Art was signed, Sundlun asked the Robbins Company of North Attleboro, Massachusetts, to bid on the inaugural medals. That company offered to make them, but at prices substantially higher than those already offered by the Medallic Art Company.

The Medallic Art Company asked that Manship deliver his models by December 12, which proved impossible. Manship came to Washington from his New York studio three times on this project. President-elect Kennedy had suggested, on his part, that the sculptor use the President's seal for the reverse. Manship studied Kennedy's face from photographs, and he then sketched several different poses for the proposed portrait. He sketched a design for the reverse as well, using the President's seal. These sketches, all merely preliminary, Manship turned over to the medals committee.

Paul Manship's sketch for the Kennedy inaugural medal
Private collection

Sundlun, familiar with inaugural and presidential traditions, noticed that the sculptor had done something extraordinary with the President's seal: the eagle's head turned toward its left, toward the arrows, not the olive branch. "What are you trying to make of Kennedy, a war President?" he asked. He took the sketches to Mrs. Kennedy, then recuperating from the birth of her son John, and he explained to her the symbolism of the eagle's head on the presidential seal. Mrs. Kennedy agreed that Manship should turn the eagle's head toward the olive branch. She also chose, from the sketches for the proposed portrait of her husband, the one she liked best.

Manship met, finally, with Kennedy on Tuesday, December 13, at the President-elect's home, 3307 N Street, in the fashionable Georgetown section of Washington. From here, Kennedy was then choosing his cabinet and other high officials for his administration, using the dining room as his headquarters. While Manship waited for his sitting from Kennedy, Mrs. Kennedy sent him word that she would like to meet him. She enormously pleased him by showing that she was familiar with his work.

Manship had only a hurried three-quarters of an hour with Kennedy. He sketched quickly. He knew his time was severely limited. The President-elect was about to leave for his family's home in Florida. He apologized for breaking off the sitting. Kennedy had posed in a good light for the artist, and Manship had his sketch, but Kennedy made a suggestion: "Why don't you come down to Florida with us?" Caught by surprise by the sudden invitation, Manship turned it down, although later he deeply regretted his hasty refusal. He could have had a great deal more time to work on his portrait of Kennedy, time he could well have used.

Manship's sketch showed Kennedy in full left profile. He submitted it to the medal design committee, chaired by John Walker, director of the National Gallery of Art. "That is pretty rapid," Manship said at the time. "Checking the studies with the subject is usually a matter of hours." Before leaving Kennedy, Manship had showed him the portrait. "O.K.," Kennedy said. "That's fine."

Manship finished his models in less than one week. He received a fee of $1,000.

By early January, the Medallic Art Company had the first medals coming off its production lines. To save money and time, the firm reduced Manship's relief on the medal by 20 percent, so that only three strikes were needed to complete the medal's

Kennedy inaugural medal
Paul Manship
Gold, 70 mm
John F. Kennedy Library

detail. Before hardening the dies, the company sent trial strikes in lead to Manship for his final approval.

As part of the promotion campaign, the company produced forty process sets of the medal, to demonstrate how the bronze medal was created. The six-piece set began with a blank planchet, showed each of the three strikes, the trimmed medal sandblasted, and finally the oxidized and finished work. These sets were sent to the sales outlets of Coin & Currency around the country for display purposes only. Although not intended for sale, these process sets eventually were sold to collectors. The company also produced forty full-size plaster reproductions of Manship's original models, and these were similarly distributed.

Sales of the medal far exceeded even Sundlun's optimistic expectations. Besides nationwide distribution for the first time, Sundlun proceeded as Gilbert Hahn had in the previous inauguration. He sent a flier to all officials of the Democratic

126

National Committee, to some thirty thousand persons who wrote in for souvenir invitations, and to an additional fifty thousand on a general invitation list. After the inauguration, Sundlun helped set up an exhibition of inaugural medals, emphasizing the Kennedy medal, at the Smithsonian Institution to further enhance sales.

Not all the sales, of course, reflected the polished sales techniques of the committee and the medal company. President Kennedy generated enormous enthusiasm among many Americans. His inaugural address excited genuine admiration throughout the world, and as a result many wanted a souvenir to mark so auspicious a beginning for a new administration.

The medals committee sold all 7,500 of the silver medals, and 53,331 in bronze, more then twice as many as were sold at either Eisenhower inauguration. These sales

(1) blank planchet   *(2) first strike*   *(3) second strike*

(4) third strike   *(5) trimmed*   *(6) polished and finished*

Process set issued by the Medallic Art Company to demonstrate how the medals were made
Richard B. Dusterberg

brought in gross revenues of $198,337.33, against costs of almost exactly $40,000. The medals committee showed a profit of $158,000! So popular was the medal that unscrupulous tricksters reproduced it in a fraudulent edition cast in cheap pot metal.

Indeed, the inauguration as a whole proved a remarkable success. The committee held no less than five inaugural balls, all heavily subscribed, but lost money on sales of parade tickets. As in 1957 and in 1953, the sale of inaugural medals had become the second most profitable venture for financing the inauguration celebration itself. The 1961 Inaugural Committee, after paying back the Guarantee Fund of $1,236,352 in full, was able to contribute $222,000 to local charities and reserved almost $48,000 for the 1965 inaugural fund.

As in the previous two inaugurations, the medals committee had the medalist strike a charm-size replica of the medal in gold for the President's wife. The committee approved additional charm-size replicas for the sculptor's wife and the wives of medals committee members.

John F. Kennedy delivering his inauguration address
U. S. Army

This year, in advance, the Medallic Art Company also produced a model for a possible inaugural medal for Richard M. Nixon in anticipation that he might win the election. Later the firm used that portrait in a medal given to Republican Party workers by Leonard W. Hall and other Nixon campaign leaders.

Almost from the first of its meetings, the inaugural medals committee discovered it had a unique and extraordinary problem: Vice President-elect Lyndon B. Johnson expected his portrait to be used along with that of President-elect Kennedy on the inaugural medal. He apparently remembered the double-portrait inaugural medal of 1957. No bashful fellow, Johnson let his wishes be known to the medal design committee, chaired by John Walker, and Walker believed the question so grave that he took it to Inaugural Committee Chairman Foley. Foley was wise to the ways of Washington and to Lyndon Johnson's mastery of backstage maneuverings. He made an appointment with Kennedy and laid the problem before the President-elect.

"Oh," Kennedy said quickly to Foley, "keep me out of this. Don't get me involved. You know what's always been done. Whatever is customary will be all right with me." Kennedy knew Johnson's vanity as well as anyone, and he simply did not want a row with Johnson on this. That is why he finessed the problem back to the committee members. Foley so reported to Walker: Kennedy wants us to do the traditional thing.

Walker therefore asked Perry B. Cott, chief curator of the National Gallery of

Art, to resolve the question. Cott made a hurried examination, using the gallery's limited collection of inaugural medals. At Walker's request, Cott reported directly to Chairman Foley: "As a rule the Vice President has not been represented on Inaugural medals. An exception is the Eisenhower medal of 1957. . . ."

Johnson, of course, did not like the decision, and he let Foley know it in his own special way, through the Washington grapevine. "I did get word from a friend of mine," Foley recounted, "that Lyndon was mad as hell that his profile was not on the medal."

Foley knew Johnson's game, and he could play it too. He told a friend in detail about the "tradition" of inaugural medals, that the portrait of the Vice President, "as a rule," was not used. He knew the friend would get the message back to Johnson. He knew that the explanation would not satisfy Johnson, but he hoped it would at least mollify any thoughts Johnson might have that the committee was deliberately prejudiced against him.

Johnson was not satisfied, nor was he mollified. He wanted his portrait on the inaugural medal, not excuses why it could not be done. At this same time, Foley had another problem—the inaugural ball committee wanted a souvenir for those attending the balls—and its solution led to solving Foley's problem with Lyndon Johnson. Mrs. Corinne Boggs, wife of the prominent Congressman from Louisiana, suggested making a charm, as a souvenir, using portraits of both Kennedy and Johnson. Foley agreed, and a contract for the souvenir charms was signed with the Robbins Company.

Johnson was a compulsive gift-giver. He constantly sought new items, with his name attached, to give away to friends and visitors, and he was delighted with the charms, even though his portrait on them was scarcely flattering. "This saved my life," he told Foley. "I've got something to give away to people." These charms, however, were not enough. He still wanted his portrait on the inaugural medal, and he let those running the inauguration know that he resented his omission. Under Johnson's continuing pressure, the Inaugural Committee decided to commission and present to him an inaugural medal of his own.

The idea came from J. Anthony Moran, a ranking official on the Inaugural Committee, and a lawyer, like Foley, wise to the Washington pressure game. Moran proposed to have a special inaugural medal made for Johnson, using the model of the charms. The committee contracted the Robbins Company to strike the medal and commissioned Philip Kraczkowski (1916—), the sculptor who had designed the charms, to make a new model on that design for the special inaugural medal for Johnson. Kraczkowski received the commission late, just before inauguration day, and it was several weeks before the finished work, struck in gold, could be presented to Johnson. The sculptor made his model from photographs sent to him at his studio in Massachusetts. Because of the lateness and to reduce expenses, Kraczkowski designed only the portrait side of the medal. Struck in the now traditional inaugural medal size of two-and-three-quarters inches, it had a blank reverse. In the left-profile portraits, Johnson appears almost as handsome as the youthful Kennedy. "The Johnsons," said Kraczkowski, "were very pleased."

Moran and others involved with this medal took the precaution of receiving for it the official sanction of the Inaugural Committee. Even though Foley had designated the Manship medal of Kennedy as "the official Inaugural souvenir," as a way of increasing sales, he also approved making this official inaugural medal for Johnson. "I did it because he was so disappointed," Foley explained. Unless it carried an official designation, it would hardly have satisfied Johnson. "It gave it credibility," Moran said.

Kennedy–Johnson charm
Philip Kraczkowski
Silver, 24 mm
Private collection

The Kennedy–Johnson medal, made expressly
for Johnson, was derived from the Kraczkowski charm.
Gold, 70 mm
Lyndon Baines Johnson Library

Some replicas of the Kraczkowski medal were struck in bronze, with blank reverses, but only one was struck in gold, the one presented to Johnson at a formal ceremony attended by Chairman Foley and other members of the Inaugural Committee. The committee did not consider striking one of these medals in gold for Kennedy, because he had already received the Manship medal struck in gold.

In the following year, the Robbins Company offered the Kraczkowski medal for sale to the public. The firm struck two thousand replicas in silver, four thousand in bronze. These differed substantially from the medal given Johnson and its replicas in bronze, for the medals sold in 1962 were not cliches, struck on only one surface. Kraczkowski designed a reverse for the commercial issue of the Kennedy–Johnson medal, using the seals of the President and Vice President. Inadvertently, the sculptor listed Johnson on that reverse as the thirty-eighth Vice President, and sixty of the medals in silver and 150 in bronze were released before the error was discovered and Johnson correctly identified as the thirty-seventh.

JFK	1961	1	(Manship-Medallic)	gold	(70 mm)	1
JFK	1961	2	(Manship-Medallic)	silver	(70 mm)	7,500
JFK	1961	3	(Manship-Medallic)	bronze	(70 mm)	53,331
JFK	1961	4	(Manship-Medallic)	gold	(27 mm)	5
JFK	1961	5	(Manship-Medallic)	gold	(24 mm)	1
JFK	1961	6	(Manship-Medallic)	gold	(21 mm)	1
JFK-LBJ	1961	1	(Kraczkowski-Robbins)	gold	(70 mm)	1
JFK-LBJ	1961	2	(Kraczkowski-Robbins)	bronze	(70 mm)	unknown

LYNDON B. JOHNSON
1965

Lyndon B. Johnson succeeded John F. Kennedy as President, on Kennedy's assassination in Dallas on November 22, 1963, and a little less than a year later, Johnson won the presidency in his own right by an overwhelming majority. Not surprisingly, Johnson wanted a full and ambitious inaugural celebration, and he named his close friend, Dale Miller, a Texan familiar with the nation's capital, as chairman of his Inaugural Committee. Miller had been Johnson's special emissary on the 1961 Inaugural Committee, and he knew what Johnson wanted without the need of being told. It was no secret that Johnson had not liked the invidious comparisons made between him and John Kennedy, and he would not brook a lesser celebration than Kennedy's.

Bruce Sundlun again wanted to chair the medals committee, and he actively sought the position, writing on his own behalf to Miller on November 13, and asking help as well from Senator John O. Pastore of Rhode Island. Miller did name Sundlun on November 20, and Sundlun went quickly to work as soon as he was appointed, naming the committee members.

On November 21, the committee sent President Johnson a special memorandum asking for his views on the inaugural medal and recommending that only his portrait be used. The memorandum also suggested using the President's seal on the reverse, as had been done in 1961, and asked Johnson whether he had a sculptor in mind to execute the medal. Aware of Johnson's intense interest in the 1961 inaugural medal, the committee was showing more than courtesy in asking for his views: it was taking a simple precaution.

Not until early December did Johnson reply to the inquiry, and then only in part. A White House staffer informed the medals committee that Johnson wished that the inaugural medal bear only the likeness of himself. He had been denied inclusion on Kennedy's inaugural medal; obviously he saw no reason to include his Vice President, Hubert Humphrey, on his inaugural medal. Johnson had not received a Kennedy medal in gold; there would be no gold Johnson medal for Humphrey either. He did receive a special version of the Johnson medal, struck in silver.

Sundlun wrote to six companies asking for bids on the medals contract. Even before he wrote, the Medallic Art Company had already asked Chairman Miller for the contract. Only one of the other companies responded to Sundlun's solicitation, and its offer was considerably higher than that of the Medallic Art Company. This year, the Medallic Art Company's bid included a guarantee of no less than $105,000 in profits. The committee had already set a target of a $200,000 profit, substantially more than the 1961 Kennedy total.

This year, Sundlun consolidated the previously scattered functions of design, contract sales, and distribution into one committee. To aid in the choice of a sculptor, Sundlun named John Walker, director of the National Gallery of Art, and his assistant, J. Carter Brown, to the committee, but they never had a chance to pick the sculptor. That had already been done by Chairman Miller.

Miller assumed he had "almost plenary powers" in his position, and simply appointed Felix de Weldon (1907—), a Washington artist best known for his gigantic statue of the United States Marines raising the flag at Iwo Jima. Miller had known de Weldon for almost twenty years. They had been next-door neighbors in a Georgetown apartment building, and de Weldon, through Miller, had come to know Lyndon and Lady Bird Johnson. "I simply chose him," Miller explained. "We'd been intimate friends for many years." De Weldon had sculpted busts of Miller's three children years before.

Miller telephoned de Weldon, and asked him to take the assignment. "Yes," de Weldon replied, "I feel honored." Later, he received a letter from the medals committee confirming the offer. De Weldon had difficulties with the committee, and they had difficulties with him. He felt he should receive $2,500 for the models. He remembered that the committee members suggested he make the models as a contribution to the inauguration and argued that "it would be wonderful publicity for me." Sundlun told de Weldon that the traditional fee had been $1,000, and that, in the end, was what he accepted.

"They suggested I work from photographs," de Weldon said. "I said I only work from photographs if the person is not alive." He telephoned Jack Valenti, one of Johnson's aides at the White House, and explained that he wanted time with the President to model his portrait. Valenti made no promises, but he said he would take the matter up with President Johnson.

On a Saturday afternoon, de Weldon received a telephone call from the White House. He was told to come immediately: the President would sit for him immediately. De Weldon hurried downtown and was promptly ushered into the Oval Office. It was just about 4 o'clock. "You can stay as long as you like," Johnson said. De Weldon had known Johnson for many years, and he felt quite comfortable with him. "It wasn't as though he was a stranger," he said. In fact, he had accepted the commission in part because he knew and admired the President. He had a theory that the very success of a portrait depended on the rapport between artist and subject. "In order to do a good portrait of a person," de Weldon explained, "you have to like him. You have to feel sympathetic. A man's face is like a diary where he writes every day."

While de Weldon worked, the President went about his presidential business. De Weldon quickly blocked out his clay-like Plasticine on a modeling board, working it into rough form. The model he fashioned was fourteen inches in diameter, abnormally large for a medal. "Then I set myself up," he said. "He was at his desk. He was very busy, especially with the telephone. I didn't mind when he had the phone on his right ear, but sometimes he had a telephone on both ears. He was telephoning all the time." That made it difficult to see his face.

De Weldon remembers working more than two hours on the portrait, and just as he was finishing it, President Johnson turned to him. "Now I'm closing up shop," he said.

"Mr. President, you want to look at it?" de Weldon asked.

"No," said Johnson, "I know you'll do the right thing."

George Reedy, the President's press secretary, came in at this point and examined de Weldon's portrait. "It looks exactly like you," he said to Johnson. Valenti came in too, and he also liked the portrait. Johnson would not look at it. Only later, when the committee presented him with the medal itself in gold did Johnson examine it, and then, said de Weldon, he studied it "very carefully."

The artist described what he had hoped to achieve in the portrait: "I wanted to

132

show the dynamic personality he was, and the love he had for the common people. In a medal you have to take just the main characteristics, because you have such a small space to work with." In the reverse, the map of the United States with the seal of the President superimposed, de Weldon found an appropriate symbolism: "The President is above all the states, the unifying power of the country. The President represents all the people."

Lyndon Johnson, often a vain man, had pronounced ideas about his looks, one of which was that the left side of his face was handsomer than the right. In his career in the Senate, he insisted that photographers snap him only from that side and never wearing his eyeglasses. Mrs. Johnson suggested to de Weldon that he model the President from his "best profile," the left. By his own account, he had no intention at any time of sculpting the President with his frequently used eyeglasses. "Eyeglasses are like a wart on the face," de Weldon said. "If a person had a wart I wouldn't put it on the medal. Eyeglasses are in addition to a face. If people can't recognize a person's features, the eyeglasses won't help."

The President's wife, Lady Bird, took a special interest in the medal. She met three times with the sculptor and members of the medals committee. At her suggestions, de Weldon substantially altered the reverse, removing an inscription he had tried and calling more dramatic attention to the states of Alaska and Hawaii. In his original model, sculpted in the Oval Office, de Weldon portrayed the President with "an open-mouth smile," and Mrs. Johnson asked him to change that to "a closed mouth, more serious and better likeness of the President."

By mid-December, de Weldon had finished his work, and the Medallic Art Company was prepared to cut the dies. Beforehand, however, plaster casts were sent to the White House for Mrs. Johnson's final approval. Then, on December 16, 1964, Chairman Dale Miller proclaimed this the official souvenir of the inauguration.

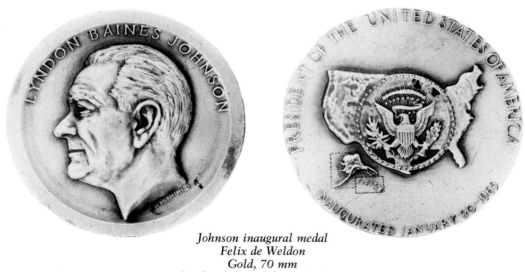

Johnson inaugural medal
Felix de Weldon
Gold, 70 mm
Lyndon Baines Johnson Library

Sundlun, well experienced from the 1961 committee, this year used two private, national firms to distribute the medals to retailers. The committee members also concentrated heavily on notifying the numismatic world that the medals were available. By Sundlun's estimate, they informed forty thousand persons in retail sales across the country about the medal. The members set up sales booths in Washington during the inauguration period. Even with a greater sales campaign than ever before, they could not sell as many medals as they had hoped, not as many as were sold four years before at the Kennedy inauguration. In 1965, Johnson had already been President for more than a year: he was not being inaugurated for the first time. His inauguration meant a continuation of programs and policies, not the excitement of a fresh beginning.

The price of silver had risen dramatically since 1961, and that caused a problem. "We were trying to keep the price the same as in 1961," Sundlun explained. "The only way to do it was to reduce the size of the silver medal." The bronze medals were struck in the now traditional size, two-and-three-quarters inches in diameter, and the silver just a little smaller, two-and-a-half inches in diameter.

The medals committee members had expected originally to sell ten thousand inaugural medals in silver and seventy thousand in bronze, from which they would net more than $200,000 in profits. They were disappointed on all counts. They sold only 26,275 in bronze and 7,695 in silver. Total gross sales amounted to $197,115 and, after costs were deducted, that left a net profit of $138,354. In all, the Inaugural Committee had spent $1,597,414, and collected enough funds, partly through the inaugural medal sales, to have $90,000 in excess of expenditures, some for charity and the rest as a reserve for the next inauguration.

Again, the medals committee ordered a small gold charm of the inaugural medal for the First Lady, and replicas of this charm were made in gold for others, including those on the medals committee. At the President's special request, the

Johnson charm, replica of the inaugural medal
Bronze, 27 mm
Private collection

committee also had the company strike a thousand of the inaugural medal charms in bronze for his personal use. "They were something for the President to give away," Sundlun explained.

LBJ	1965	1	gold	(70 mm)	1
LBJ	1965	2	silver	(70 mm)	1
LBJ	1965	3	silver	(64 mm)	7,695
LBJ	1965	4	bronze	(70 mm)	26,275
LBJ	1965	5	bronze	(27 mm)	1,000
LBJ	1965	6	gold	(27 mm)	9

RICHARD M. NIXON
1969

In the presidential election of 1968, Richard M. Nixon narrowly defeated Hubert H. Humphrey, and within days after the election, Nixon's friends and colleagues were planning an inauguration for him, the like of which had never been seen before. Nixon chose J. Willard Marriott, wealthy owner of a restaurant chain, as Chairman of the Inaugural Committee. The committee Marriott assembled planned a massive parade and no less than six balls at various hotels in Washington. They also planned a gala and a concert of ambitious proportions. On November 18, Marriott telephoned Dr. Melvin Payne of the National Geographic Society and asked him to accept the chairmanship of the medals committee. This would be no ordinary exercise. The celebrations already at the planning stage would cost a small fortune. The Guarantee Fund raised $2,182,000 to underwrite the celebration, and there would be extraordinary pressures to pay the costs of the celebrations and to repay those subscribing to the Guarantee Fund. In the past four inaugurations, the medals committee had proved that the inaugural medal could be used to raise substantial funds to defray other costs. That would be its prime role this year.

Payne, however, was a man of parts, not content merely to use the medal as a money-raiser. Familiar with the techniques and practices of making medals, he knew from the start that he wanted to select "an outstanding artist," to agree upon an appropriate design, and to "execute the design as quickly as was compatible with artistic excellence." He knew the needs to raise funds with this medal, to sell replicas of it far and wide; but his first concern was for artistic excellence. As a result, the first person he appointed to his committee was John Walker, Director of the National Gallery of Art. Payne and Walker held a meeting on November 22, to consider which artist they would commission. Payne had asked William Louth, president of the Medallic Art Company, to join them and to bring with him samples of medals designed by several outstanding contemporary sculptors. Among the medals examined were works by Frank Gasparro, Walker Hancock, C. Paul Jennewein, Ralph J. Menconi, Felix de Weldon, Spiro Anargyros, and Joseph Kisselawski. The group agreed that Jennewein, Hancock, and Menconi were particularly well qualified because, as Payne reported, "All of them worked reasonably fast and this, of course, was essential." They decided, however, that Nixon should make the final decision.

They also decided not to ask President-elect Nixon to sit for the sculptor chosen, but to have the sculptor work from up-to-date portrait photographs.

"It was our view," Payne stated in his report, "that a three-quarter view would be desirable." This was a matter of delicacy, not to be mentioned in any public way, but those responsible for making the Nixon medal believed that a three-quarter-view portrait of Nixon would allow the sculptor to de-emphasize his nose. Until now, every presidential inaugural medal had been a portrait in full profile, but a full profile of Nixon was not what the committee wanted. In due course, the sculptor selected was so informed, and tried to modify his portrait accordingly.

Immediately after this meeting, Payne telephoned to ask for an appointment with Nixon as soon as possible, sending word to the President-elect that photographs for the medalist had to be taken promptly, "since personal sittings were out of the question." Nixon agreed to meet with Payne, Louth, and two photographers at his headquarters in New York City at the Hotel Pierre, the very next afternoon, November 23. After fully examining the samples of the three proposed sculptors, Nixon chose Menconi (1915–1972). Payne discussed with Nixon how he wished to be portrayed, and he agreed to a three-quarter view of the right side of his face. "Nixon," said Payne, "does not have a good profile."

At this meeting, no decision was made on the design for the reverse of the medal. Nixon asked for time to think about that. Two days later, on November 25, he sent word to Payne that, if possible, he would like the sculptor to use a crewelwork pattern of the Great Seal of the United States that his daughter Julie had made and presented to him on election night as a surprise. Beneath the seal, Julie Nixon had embroidered "To RN JN."

Sculptor Menconi was already at work. Payne had commissioned him, as soon as Nixon chose him, for a fee of $1,500, and the photographs reached him at his New York studio the same day Nixon decided to use Julie's crewelwork for the reverse. Payne promptly notified Menconi of Nixon's wish. "He liked that as a way to personalize the medal," Payne explained. "We enthusiastically supported it."

At a meeting of the medals committee on November 29, the members voted to give the contract for the medal to the Medallic Art Company. Explaining that decision, Payne said in his report: "They were the leading organization in this field, had a fine reputation for quality and integrity, and were fully experienced." The company had made inaugural medals for Presidents Coolidge, Roosevelt, Eisenhower, Kennedy, and Johnson. The committee considered no other firm. There was no competition.

The committee also decided that the inaugural medals would be struck in both bronze and silver for public sale—two-and-three-quarters inches for the bronze, two-and-a-half inches for the silver. The members decided to limit the silver medals to fifteen thousand at $45 each, and to sell the bronze medals in an unlimited edition at $6.00 each.

An outstanding medalist, noted for his ability to sculpt full-face medallic portraits successfully, Menconi completed the Plasticine models of the obverse and reverse in two weeks. He cast these in plaster, and took them to Nixon for his approval at a curious interview, in the President-elect's headquarters at the Hotel Pierre.

Menconi set up his models and waited, but a Nixon aide asked him to leave so that the President-elect could examine the studies privately. After a short wait, Menconi was asked to return to meet Nixon. "That's great," Nixon said to him. "I like it very much."

Once approved, the master models were reduced to dies at the Medallic Art Company, and the first shipment of medals reached Washington shortly after the beginning of the new year.

Meanwhile, the committee had launched an extraordinary campaign to sell the medals in unprecedented quantities. As other recent inaugural medals committees had done, this committee contracted with two major wholesale distributors to sell silver and bronze medals through their outlets nationwide. These two distributors alone returned a net royalty income of almost $150,000. The committee also arranged to have the medals sold at banks and various other places in the nation's capital and, of course, by mail order.

The committee also undertook an energetic publicity campaign, and concentrated on newspapers, magazines, and radio and television stations throughout the country. "Our publicity," reported Chairman Payne, "was beyond our most optimistic expectations and contributed tremendously to our sales effort." The press printed many articles about the medal, and it appeared on the cover of *Time* magazine in the issue of inauguration week.

The sales proved phenomenal. All fifteen thousand of the silver medals were sold by inauguration day, and the medals committee twice rejected a proposal to increase the striking of the silver medals. In all, there were 78,529 bronze medals sold. Never before had an inaugural medal sold in such numbers, or brought in so much revenue. Its sales grossed $684,338.96—a staggering sum—and the total production cost to the committee was $229,618.15. This meant a profit of $454,720.81. That was almost half of the $949,000 the Inaugural Committee had left in excess revenue after paying off its total expenses of $2,762,000. It donated $672,000 to various charities and retained $328,000 for the next Inaugural Committee.

"This," said Chairman Payne in his report, "is far and away the most successful medal operation in history. . . ." Only the inaugural balls brought in more profits than the Nixon medals. As Chairman Payne reported to the Inaugural Committee, he could have sold a great many more medals with an earlier start. Clearly, the inaugural medals had become an enormously consequential part of the entire inaugural celebrations, themselves producing enough income to finance a century of inaugurations of the past.

The medals committee directed the Medallic Art Company to strike a two-and-three-quarter-inch medal in gold, and this was presented to President Nixon on May 7. It also had the company strike a special version of the medal for Vice President

Nixon inaugural medal
Ralph J. Menconi
Silver, 64 mm
Private collection

Spiro Agnew, which was two-and-three-quarters inches, struck in silver and, like the gold medal for the President, a unique piece. "It was the difference between the general and the captain," Payne said, explaining why Agnew received a silver medal, not a gold. "Rank has its privileges."

Nixon clichés in presentation box
Private collection

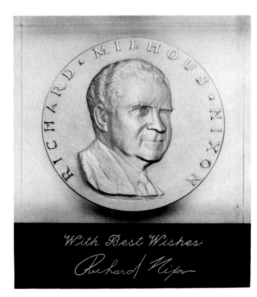

Nixon presentation piece
Private collection

Nixon paperweight
Private collection

    At the request of the State Department, the committee authorized the striking of a special variant of the medal for use by the Protocol Office. These were one-and-a-half inches in diameter, struck in bronze, and encased in lucite so that they could be used as paperweights. They were presented to distinguished foreign visitors.

    At the President's request, the company struck 1,100 sets of bronze clichés of the two-and-three-quarter-inch medal, and most of these were mounted in walnut frames, as gifts for Nixon to give congressional and other influential friends. At the White House's request, five hundred bronze medals were gold-plated and encased in lucite, with a greeting from Nixon and his signature stamped in gold at the base.

These, also, he gave away. Inaugural Committee Chairman Marriott had approximately a hundred similarly made, but with his own signature, as gifts to his friends and colleagues.

The company struck five gold charms of this medal in gold, one-and-three-sixteenths inches in diameter, for presentation to Mrs. Nixon and the wives of some committee officials. It made an even smaller obverse die, similar to the inaugural medal's obverse, which was only about the size of a dime. This was used to strike small replicas in bronze, silver, and gold, for use on such jewelry items as tie clips and cuff links.

Nixon tie clip
Private collection

RMN	1969	1	gold	(70 mm)	1
RMN	1969	2	silver	(70 mm)	1
RMN	1969	3	silver	(64 mm)	15,000
RMN	1969	4	bronze	(70 mm)	78,529
RMN	1969	5	bronze	(38 mm)	1,000
RMN	1969	6	gold-plated bronze in lucite (70 mm)		500
RMN	1969	7	silver uniface cliché (70 mm) obverse		3
RMN	1969	8	silver uniface cliché (70 mm) reverse		3
RMN	1969	9	bronze uniface cliché (70 mm) obverse		1,100
RMN	1969	10	bronze uniface cliché (70 mm) reverse		1,100
RMN	1969	11	gold	(29 mm)	5

RICHARD M. NIXON
1973

In November 1972, President Nixon and Vice President Agnew won reelection by a smashing majority, with Massachusetts the only state voting for their opponents. As far as their admirers were concerned, this extraordinary victory margin called for an extraordinary celebration at the inauguration. Again, President Nixon asked J. Willard Marriott, his friend, to serve as Chairman of the Inaugural Committee. Marriott planned the most expansive and elaborate inauguration ever held for an American President. Unlike the previous inauguration, this one would be largely directed by the White House staff and those who had helped reelect Nixon and Agnew as workers for the Committee to Reelect the President, sometimes called CREEP.

There was no rush to appoint a medals committee. Marriott asked Dr. Payne to assume again the chairmanship, but Payne declined. He did offer to advise on making the new inaugural medal, but those in charge chose not to seek his help.

The negotiations for the medal contract began within days after the election, and this year a relatively new private mint, the Franklin Mint, actively sought the contract, in competition with the Medallic Art Company. The Franklin Mint, founded in 1964 by Joseph M. Segel, had shown extraordinary growth and profits in merchandising proof-finished, low-relief medals, usually issued in extensive sets.

Under Segel, the firm was aggressive and almost startlingly active. Segel, for example, negotiated a contract with the White House Historical Association under which the firm produced a series of medals to be sold at the White House. The Historical Society received 10 percent of gross sales, with a guaranteed minimum payment of $200,000. That arrangement brought considerable public criticism from those who believed the White House should not be involved in such commercial ventures.

When Segel approached the White House and Marriott's Inaugural Committee for the medals contract, he was already well known to both groups. Significantly, Segel himself had contributed $113,000 in Franklin Mint stock to the reelection committee for Richard M. Nixon. This was an extraordinarily large gift, even in that year of extraordinarily large gifts to Nixon's reelection committee. Those initiated in such matters could guess that Nixon's campaign managers had "assessed" Segel for a substantial gift, taking into account his contract for the White House medals, and that Segel himself would feel he had special access to the Nixon White House in the years to come.

That reasoning applied, specifically, to the inaugural medal for 1973. Over the years since 1953, the concept of striking inaugural medals had grown increasingly commercial, and now seeking the contract was the most aggressively commercial mint in the country. The Medallic Art Company over its years had remained somewhat staid and correct, making its compromises on high-relief medals occasionally, but insisting that its function was the manufacture of art objects, not commercial factory products. Its managers could only look askance at the tactics of the Franklin Mint and regret its startling financial successes.

In preparation for the negotiations, the Medallic Art Company commissioned Eleanor Platt (1910–1974), a distinguished sculptor, to design and model a medal with the double portraits of President Nixon and Vice President Agnew. The firm's chief negotiator, William Louth, had this model in plaster from the artist as the negotiations, or rather the bidding, got under way in early December.

Moreover, Louth had prepared a special presentation book, bound in brown imitation leather, with the Nixon 1969 medal embedded in the cover, to make his company's case for the contract. The book emphasized that Medallic Art had made the inaugural medal for Nixon in 1969 even more than it argued for Eleanor Platt's new model.

Medallic Art, in the fierce competition with the Franklin Mint, had scrambled to come up with new ideas. The firm proposed striking an inaugural plate, using the models for the inaugural medal as its central feature. It suggested minting inaugural medals in partial gold (gold fill), inasmuch as higher-grade gold could not then be legally sold. The gold-filled medals would measure two inches in diameter, by Medallic's proposal, and sell for $125 each. The firm offered as well, of course, the now traditional inaugural medals in bronze and silver in the accustomed sizes.

On its part, the Franklin Mint proposed not only an inaugural plate, struck in silver, but four different inaugural medals—of bronze and silver, each in antique and proof finish. The firm specialized in proof-finished medals, a style Medallic Art had never attempted.

Negotiating for the Inaugural Committee was Chairman Marriott and a small group of White House aides, led by Michael Raoul Duval. There were no members of the medals committee involved.

Under the pressure of the Franklin Mint's competition, Louth offered figures suggesting that the Medallic Art proposal could possibly net the Inaugural Committee $967,500. This assumed that the company and the committee could sell two thousand gold-filled medals at $125 each, fifty thousand silver medals at $60 each, a hundred thousand bronze medals at $8.50 each, and two thousand silver inaugural plates (measuring eight inches) at $200 each. They were ambitious estimates, far in excess of the 1969 figures, and Marriott had a right to feel skeptical.

The Franklin Mint had no less than five sculptors prepare models for the 1973 Nixon–Agnew inaugural medal. President Nixon had indicated that he would like Agnew's portrait included for this second medal, as he himself had been on Eisenhower's. Each of the five sculptors—Gilroy Roberts, James Ferrell, Harold Faulkner, Richard Baldwin, and Vincent Miller—had obviously copied from the same original. Their designs were all but identical, with only Miller's at all in variance with the others. They seem to have all used as their model a medal earlier sculpted by Roberts, for each of the models looks like an exact copy of his 1970 medal for the Republican National Committee, a double profile of Nixon and Agnew. None of the sculptors, of course, had modelled Nixon or Agnew from life for these medals.

Roberts had once modelled Nixon from life, a mere fifteen minutes, but that was for a different medal. He put little value in personal sittings and normally modelled his medals from photographs. "You're lucky to get any time with the President," he said. "It's a ritual to be able to say you were there. You don't get much work done with people coming and going."

The Franklin Mint had gone to the trouble of making dies for each of the five versions of the Nixon–Agnew portrait and then struck them in both bronze and silver, with one of each in antique finish and one of each in proof finish. In sum, the Franklin Mint submitted four trial strikes from each of the five sculptors, twenty examples in all. Franklin proposed selling the antique silver medals for $45 each, those in proof for $50, and the antique bronze medals for $6 each, those in proof for $10. Their proposal, 20 percent of gross sales, amounted to a higher potential return for the Inaugural Committee than Medallic offered.

Clearly, Franklin had the distinct advantage in this bidding. Hard pressed, Medallic's Louth finally offered the committee a cash guarantee of $750,000 with half of that amount to be paid thirty days after sales of the medals began.

Segel, for the Franklin Mint, offered a guarantee of $1,000,000 to the Inaugural Committee, payable immediately. He had a bank check in that amount with him which he handed to Willard Marriott. It was a stunning offer.

That ended the competition: Marriott was delighted. He had assured the Inaugural Committee of $1,000,000—more than double the return of the 1969 medal, more profit than had been received by all the previous Inaugural Committees combined from the sale of inaugural medals. "Remember we have no government subsidy," Marriott said, "so we must bring home the bacon."

The negotiations, not surprisingly, had been purely commercial. No concern had been shown by Marriott or the Nixon aides for the merit of the medals to be produced under this contract. The hard bargaining had been about cash. "We have no reason to believe that the decision was based on anything other than a fair competitive analysis," Louth said after the announcement that the Franklin Mint had received the contract. "If the primary function of the Inaugural Committee is to raise money, it may have made the right decision." Marriott defended the decision. "The decision to award this contract was based on quality, service, and price," he said. "We believe the Franklin Mint will create a medal of unexcelled quality."

Chosen for the design to be used was the model by Gilroy Roberts (1905—). "We had a pretty aggressive group," he said later. The sculptor explained that his firm had much more in mind than just a cash return from receiving this contract. In fact, the offer was far in excess of what purely businesslike practicality would allow.

Nixon–Agnew inaugural medal
Gilroy Roberts
Silver, 63 mm
Private collection

The Franklin Mint was new and suddenly rich, but it lacked reputation and stature. Segel was seeking these with this contract, and he had ambitions of his own. "We wanted it for the prestige, the recognition, and the publicity," Roberts said. Under the contract, the Franklin Mint handled everything: design, production, publicity, and delivery. The Inaugural Committee had little more to do than deposit the check for $1,000,000. It was pure profit.

Only belatedly did Marriott appoint a medals committee, and the members had nothing to do. The contract had already been awarded, the medal already approved. One of those named to the medals committee was Darrell C. Crain, Jr., son of the designer of the 1917, 1921, and 1925 inaugural medals. He was bitter at the exclusion of his committee from the decision-making: *Whereas former committees had consisted of prominent citizens dedicated to ensuring the striking of a true work of art,* he later wrote, *the 1973 medals committee turned out to be a 'paper committee' appointed after all decisions had been made by a small council from the official circle whose primary interest appeared to be financial. The result was as might be expected: a million dollars for the Inaugural Committee, but a medal which is far from spectacular.* In fact, it was of uninspired design, struck in low relief. It marked the ultimate in the commercialization of the inaugural medal. It was a far cry from the medal that Theodore Roosevelt had asked Augustus Saint-Gaudens to design.

The Franklin Mint merchandised this inaugural medal as none had been before. The company took full-page advertisements in major newspapers across the country. It sent special order forms to its own extensive list of collectors, and sold more inaugural medals than ever before: 16,302 in proof silver, 6,860 in antique silver, 49,789 in proof bronze, and 56,574 in antique bronze. The company sold 10,483 silver inaugural plates at $150 each. Gross receipts to the company amounted to slightly more than $3,533,000. On the basis of its offer of 20 percent of gross, the company would have paid the Inaugural Committee a little more than $700,000, almost $300,000 less than the amount it actually paid. The Inaugural Committee showed a slight profit on total expenditures, for the celebration, of more than $3,500,000.

The Franklin Mint made no charm-sized inaugural medals, as had been done by the Medallic Art Company since 1953. The Inaugural Committee presented gold medals to President Nixon and Vice President Agnew. As in 1969, again at the request of the White House, seven hundred of the bronze medals were gold-plated and mounted in lucite, with a greeting from President Nixon and a replica of his signature stamped in gold at the base. Similarly, Chairman Marriott also had made a hundred of these with his greeting and signature as gifts for friends and committee colleagues.

Pleased with the Eleanor Platt portrait of Nixon, the Medallic Art Company's officers had it reduced to a die, first removing the portrait of Agnew, and had some copies struck in bronze. In these medals, the company mixed the Platt portrait of Nixon with the reverse of the 1969 inaugural medal.

RMN	1973	1	gold	(70 mm)	2
RMN	1973	2	proof silver	(63 mm)	16,302
RMN	1973	3	antique silver	(63 mm)	6,860
RMN	1973	4	proof bronze	(70 mm)	49,789
RMN	1973	5	antique bronze	(70 mm)	56,574
RMN	1973	6	gold-plated bronze in lucite	(70 mm)	700

Silver inaugural plate
Private collection

An adaptation of the Medallic Art Company's
proposed inaugural medal. It was suggested
that Nixon could use these as presentation pieces.
Bronze, 70 mm
Private collection

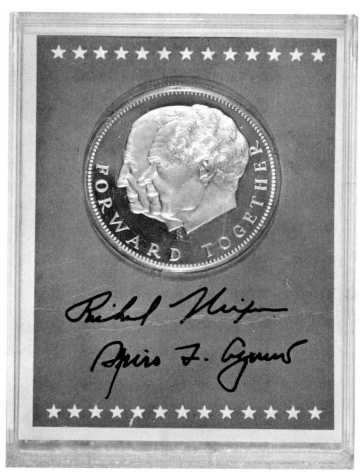

Nixon–Agnew "Forward Together" presentation medal
Silver, 39 mm
Private collection

GERALD R. FORD

(VICE PRESIDENT)

1973

On October 10, 1973, Vice President Spiro Agnew resigned, and pleaded *nolo contendere* to criminal charges brought against him in a federal court. Under the provisions of the United States Constitution's Twenty-Fifth Amendment, adopted in 1967, President Nixon thereupon nominated Congressman Gerald R. Ford of Michigan to become the next Vice President. That required the approval of both houses of the Congress. This was the first time these constitutional provisions had been used, and Ford received the nomination under even more extraordinary circumstances than the resignation of Vice President Agnew. President Nixon himself was under investigation by a Senate committee and a special federal prosecutor, Archibald Cox, on allegations that he had violated federal law. Therefore, the Senate and the House of Representatives took special caution in examining Ford: he well could become President if Nixon, like Agnew, were forced to resign.

Hard pressed by Cox for certain recordings of his conversations at the White House, Nixon resolved to rid himself of this antagonist. He ordered Cox fired and the special prosecutor's office abolished. Then his attorney general and deputy attorney general resigned in protest, and in a matter of days Nixon appeared in serious danger of being cited for contempt by a federal court. The city of Washington was in turmoil, and Nixon seemed in greater political danger than ever. In the midst of these events, this writer visited Ford at his Capitol office. I told him that, in my judgment, the events under way would eventually force the resignation or removal of Nixon, and that Ford should begin preparing himself to succeed to that office. In the course of our conversation, we speculated about Ford's course in these unique circumstances. If he became President, that oath-taking would be classified as an official inauguration, and I suggested it might be an appropriate time to strike an inaugural medal to mark the occasion. Ford had not before heard of inaugural medals, and he was curious about their tradition.

A few days later, I visited Senator Mark O. Hatfield of Oregon, also a medal enthusiast, and told him about my idea of striking an inaugural medal for a President Ford. Hatfield immediately liked the idea, but we both knew that no such medal could be prepared, nor even openly discussed, with President Nixon still in the White House. Hatfield puzzled over that for a moment. "I have it!" Hatfield said. "We'll strike an 'interim' medal. We'll strike a medal for Ford becoming Vice President. He will be the first Vice President under the 25th Amendment." The presidential inaugural medal for Ford could come later.

The next day, I telephoned the Medallic Art Company to ask whether the firm would be interested in striking a Vice Presidential inaugural medal for Gerald Ford. The firm's officials were excited by the idea, but they cited requirements for such a project. The most important was that the Vice President-designate had to give his "sanction," or the medal could not be considered official. A special committee would have to be created to commission the medal, to oversee its making, and to distribute the royalties as Ford would designate.

I went to see Ford again, and at first he rejected the idea. It sounded too self-serving, he said, too self-promotional. I told him that it was not he who would commission the medals, that this would be done by a special committee, but that the committee could not act without his permission. "All right," Ford said at last, "but keep it in good hands."

I suggested Senator Hatfield as chairman, and Ford approved. Ford said he would also like, as members of the committee, Michigan's two United States Senators, Philip A. Hart and Robert Griffin, and Elford Cederberg, the senior member of the Michigan delegation in the House of Representatives. Ford considered several options for the royalties and decided on a scholarship fund at the University of Michigan, of which he was a graduate.

There was no time to lose, no time even for Ford to sit for a sculptor. He agreed, somewhat reluctantly, to pose for photographs for the sculptor. He had been so busy testifying during that period that he had not had time to go to a barber; and his hair was longer than he liked it. "I'll tell the sculptor to give you a haircut," I promised him.

Hatfield, a take-charge fellow, put the committee together with great speed. On the day Ford agreed to create the inaugural medals committee, the Senate confirmed him as Vice President. The House of Representatives was scheduled to do the same only nine days later, on December 6. Hatfield notified the Michigan congressmen that Ford wanted them to serve. He also invited Elvira Clain-Stefanelli, curator of the Smithsonian's numismatics division, and Michael Radock, Vice President of the University of Michigan.

In traditional terms, the medals committee thus created was unique, but it closely resembled the committee put together by Ambassador Davies for President Roosevelt's wartime inauguration in 1945. That group had also operated alone, without a parent Inaugural Committee. It had no celebration to help finance; it existed solely to commission an inaugural medal.

The Medallic Art Company put staff artists immediately to work to sketch proposed reverses for the medal. After some discussion, the firm chose Romanian-born sculptor Mico Kaufman (1924—), who could immediately take the assignment. The committee members had no thought but that the Medallic Art Company should strike this medal. They, of course, wanted a design in high relief. The Ford medals were to be part of the presidential inaugural tradition, in the standard sizes of two-and-three-quarters inches for the bronze and two-and-a-half inches for the silver. At first, officials at the Medallic Art Company balked at making two sizes, reluctant to spend the money for an extra set of dies, but on second thought they agreed readily enough.

On December 3, just a week after Hatfield had come up with the idea of a vice-presidential inaugural medal, the president of the Medallic Art Company, William Louth, came to Washington to meet the committee members. He had drafted an agreement which, after some discussion, the committee members accepted. Under that agreement, the committee authorized five different versions of the Ford inaugural medal for sale to the public: (1) an unlimited edition of the medal, two-and-three-quarters inches in diameter, in bronze, (2) an edition of 2,500 medals, two-and-a-half inches in diameter, in antique finished silver; (3) another 2,500 medals, two-and-a-half inches in diameter, in proof silver; (4) an edition of a thousand medals,

Ford University of Michigan medal
Proof bronze, 38 mm
Private collection

two-and-a-half inches in diameter, in vermeil (gold-plated silver); and (5) a special unlimited edition of a variation of the medal, in low relief, one-and-a-half inches in diameter, in proof silver. The small medal was designated the "University of Michigan medal," in the expectation of selling many of them to Ford's fellow alumni. The Medallic Art Company had never before contracted to make medals in proof finish, but did so now only because of the Franklin Mint's remarkable financial success with them, including the 1973 Nixon inaugural medals.

Meanwhile, Mico Kaufman worked on his models. He did not know Ford, but he was told that Ford was a serious-minded, unostentatious man, gregarious, candid, and still with the rugged physique of a once powerful athlete. The private mint's artists had sketched a half dozen suggestions for the reverse, and Senator Hatfield asked Ford to select the one he liked. From these, Ford chose a design showing the vice-presidential seal superimposed on the Capitol's dome. Kaufman worked up the reverse from that sketch. For the portrait, Kaufman modelled an effigy of a man with a square, jutting jaw, seemingly almost defiant. Hatfield objected to the original plaster model: Kaufman had made Ford look too jowly. He asked that the jaw line be trimmed and corrected, which Kaugman did. Then he took the models to Ford for his approval before permitting the company to proceed.

Ford inaugural medal trial strikes
Private collection

148

By mid-December, Ford had approved the models, and Hatfield told the company to proceed. On December 16, the company released photographs of Kaufman's designs and announced, as well, that Ford had authorized this as the official medal commemorating his inauguration as Vice President. The company had arranged for three regional distributors to wholesale some of the medals, but the private mint itself sold the bulk of the medals directly to the public.

By early January, the Medallic Art Company had completed the hardening of the two-and-a-half-inch dies intended for the silver medals, and struck ten medals in bronze from these dies for members of the company's board of governors. By mid-January, it had struck and finished the inaugural medal in gold for Ford, and on January 21, Senator Hatfield, accompanied by the sculptor and members of his committee, presented it to Vice President Ford in his formal office at the Capitol just off the Senate chamber. Ford liked the medals. He placed them on display in his home in Alexandria, Virginia. "They are beautiful," he scribbled in a note to a member of the committee, "and the next time you are in the home you will see how proudly we display them."

Not surprisingly, the gold-plated silver medals, limited to a numbered edition of only a thousand, sold out quickly. The medals struck in proof silver were also popular, and sold out by late spring. There was least demand for the silver medals in antique finish, and by the time they were sold out completely in the edition of 2,500, Ford had become President, and Hatfield's committee had started work on a new series of presidential inaugural medals for him. The company sold 10,484 of the vice-presidential medals in bronze and 11,151 of the small, low-relief medals in proof silver.

Ford Vice-Presidential inaugural medal
Mico Kaufman
Gold, 63 mm
The President and Mrs. Gerald R. Ford

GRF	1973	1	gold	(63 mm)	1
GRF	1973	2	vermeil	(63 mm)	1,000
GRF	1973	3	proof silver	(63 mm)	2,500
GRF	1973	4	antique silver	(63 mm)	2,500
GRF	1973	5	bronze	(70 mm)	10,484
GRF	1973	6	bronze	(63 mm)	10
GRF	1973	7	proof silver	(38 mm)	11,151
GRF	1973	8	proof bronze	(38 mm)	1

GERALD R. FORD

1974

In late July, 1974, the judiciary committee of the House of Representatives voted decisively to impeach President Nixon for high crimes and misdemeanors. Rather than face trial and certain conviction by the United States Senate, Nixon resigned as President on August 9. Vice President Gerald R. Ford promptly took the oath of office as the succeeding President, in a moving ceremony at the White House.

Even before Nixon's resignation, those most significantly involved with Ford's vice-presidential medal were discussing the medal for his inauguration as President. Indeed, the idea of striking this medal had led, initially, to striking a medal for his inauguration as Vice President. The chief officer of the Medallic Art Company at first believed that the somber circumstances of Nixon's resignation made it inappropriate to strike a medal for Ford, but Senator Mark Hatfield thought differently. So did members of the Ford vice presidential inaugural medals committee.

By chance, Senator Hatfield had been invited to a state dinner at the White House for King Hussein of Jordan, but Nixon's sudden resignation had made Ford the President and the host at this dinner. Meeting Ford there, Hatfield asked his permission to strike an official medal marking his inauguration as President. Ford agreed immediately. Hatfield telephoned a member of the medals committee the next morning. "We're back in business," he said.

This time, however, the committee confronted a situation far different from that with the vice-presidential medal. For one thing, the change in Presidents had created great confusion within the White House staff structure, making it difficult to get prompt decisions. The President's new men tended, as well, to be cautious and protective about anything involving him, and they were reluctant to speak or act for him. Moreover, other firms now took an interest in striking a Ford inaugural medal, and one, the Franklin Mint, campaigned vigorously backstage to win the contract. That firm had struck the Nixon medals in 1973, and it now threw all its influence into this effort. J. Willard Marriott, chairman of the Nixon Inaugural Committees of 1969 and 1973, became that firm's principal spokesman in these high-level negotiations. Repeatedly they made overtures, not to President Ford, who was too busy for such matters, but to the chief of his White House staff, General Alexander Haig.

Haig saw, in this pressure from the Franklin Mint, the possibility of difficulty for the new President, and he telephoned Senator Hatfield on several occasions, urging him to solve the problem. Haig relayed to him the proposals so urgently pressed by the Franklin Mint. That firm was suggesting not only a repetition of the different types of inaugural medals, in proof and antique finished silver and bronze, but also an inaugural plate similar to the one made for Nixon's inauguration in 1973. In their arguments to General Haig, the Franklin Mint officials emphasized their ability to manufacture a product that would generate substantial profits. From their contract in 1973, they had produced $1,000,000 toward the funding of that inauguration. "We have a very informal committee," Hatfield explained to General Haig.

"Our purpose is not to raise money to pay other inauguration expenses. It's merely an extension of the previously authorized medal."

Haig obviously wanted the problem solved with a minimum of fuss. "It's totally up to the committee," he told Senator Hatfield.

Hatfield had an idea on how to blunt the pressure from the Franklin Mint: he would add to the committee's roster an advocate for that firm. Again Hatfield consulted with fellow committee members, and then he asked Willard Marriott to serve on the medals committee too.

Meanwhile, the Medallic Art Company had formulated proposals of its own for the Ford presidential medal. These were submitted to Hatfield on August 20, just eleven days after Ford had become President. The firm suggested again striking limited editions of the medal in silver and an unlimited edition in bronze, in the now traditional sizes, but also suggested a small version in gold, when it became legal to market gold medals. Legislation to this purpose already seemed certain of passage by Congress.

Hatfield called a meeting of the medals committee on September 6, in his office in the Senate Office Building. Marriott had wanted to bring a representative of the Franklin Mint to the meeting, but Hatfield suggested instead that he present its case at the meeting. This Marriott did.

"If there's going to be a medal," he told the committee members, "my only interest is to have a good one and to sell as many as you can." He told of his experience with the 1973 inaugural medals and the Franklin Mint. "We put that out on bids," said Marriott. "They sent in a check for $1 million and a percentage above a certain amount. I have a lot of experience selling these things and an interest in seeing that the President gets the most money he can out of them. These guys are real promoters. I think everything last time was first class."

Mrs. Elvira Clain-Stefanelli, curator of the Smithsonian's numismatics division, responded to Marriott's argument. She explained that this committee had no need to raise money for any purpose: there were no inauguration ceremonies that needed funding. Rather, she said, the committee had the opportunity to commission a medal marking an historic moment in the nation's history. That medal, she said, would endure, as medals do, and five hundred years from now it would be looked at as the commemorative of this presidential inauguration. The committee, she argued, should bend every effort to create a medal worthy of the event it commemorated, a medal of greatest possible artistic merit.

Clearly, the committee members supported Mrs. Clain-Stefanelli's argument, and there was no question but that the Medallic Art Company was the committee's overwhelming choice. Senator Hatfield understood as well as anyone in politics the need to cushion losses to losers and the ways to do it. He mentioned now that the Franklin Mint proposed an inaugural plate, an item in which the Medallic Art Company had no interest, and suggested that the Franklin Mint make a plate from the design approved for the Medallic Art Company. That would somewhat divide the benefits, and it would ease the minds of those at the White House concerned about the Franklin Mint. The committee quickly adopted Hatfield's suggestion.

The Medallic Art Company had asked two sculptors to offer models for President Ford's portrait. One of these was Mico Kaufman, who had modelled Ford's vice-presidential inauguration medal. The other was Abram Belskie. Kaufman submitted a new portrait of Ford. He was not pleased with it, however, and, despite the press for time, he modelled still another. He portrayed the President as a sensi-

Ford inaugural medal
Mico Kaufman and Frank Eliscu
Gold, 63 mm
The President and Mrs. Gerald R. Ford

tive man, deep in thought, and it was this portrait that the medals committee unanimously chose.

For the reverse of the medal, the company submitted several sketches, none of which caught the fancy of the committee. At the suggestion of the company, another sculptor, Frank Eliscu, modelled the reverse. Eliscu had sculpted a soaring eagle, a dramatic and vivid work, which the Medallic Art Company had given to President Ford. The committee asked that Eliscu use that same eagle on the medal's reverse.

This was not the first time that different sculptors worked together on presidential inaugural medals, but in the Ford medal there was not the jarring conflict between obverse and reverse which had marred Franklin Roosevelt's 1941 medal. Kaufman's rugged portrait of Ford suggested the strength of the man, and Eliscu's powerful eagle enhanced that impression by suggesting the power of the presidency too. Eliscu also used the presidential seal on the reverse, as had been done in all presidential inaugural medals since that for John Kennedy, but the sculptor made the seal subservient to his larger symbolism.

On October 3, President Ford approved the models. The committee ordered three versions in silver: silver vermeil in an edition of 2,500; proof silver in an edition of five thousand, and antique silver in an edition of 7,500. As customary, the edition of bronze medals was unlimited. The company sold far less than those authorized: 2,075 in silver vermeil, 3,247 in proof silver, and only 2,330 in antique silver. It sold 13,664 bronze medals. At President Ford's request, the royalties went to cancer research.

The committee also authorized the striking of twelve silver medals, measuring two-and-three-quarters inches. These went to members of the committee. On December 10, Senator Hatfield presented to President Ford the one gold medal authorized. At the same time, he presented a charm-size replica of her husband's medal to Mrs. Ford. The First Lady's gold charm actually was one of two trial pieces, one in antique finish, the other in proof-like finish. On October 28, the medals committee met in Senator Hatfield's office and approved the striking of fifteen hundred medals in eighteen-karat gold, for sale when they became legal to sell, on January 1, 1975. Later, the committee increased that number to 1,550, all of which were sold.

The Franklin Mint offered the official inaugural plate to collectors in sterling silver, with proof finish, at $200 each, and in eighteen-karat gold, also proof finish, at $3,500 each. The firm sold ten of the plates in gold and 1,130 in silver.

In June 1975, the Medallic Art Company, despite the copyright, used the reverse of the Ford inaugural for a special medal that it suggested the President have on hand to give away during the country's bicentennial year.

GRF	1974	1	gold	(63 mm)	1
GRF	1974	2	gold	(32 mm)	1,551
GRF	1974	3	vermeil	(63 mm)	2,075
GRF	1974	4	proof silver	(63 mm)	3,247
GRF	1974	5	antique silver	(63 mm)	2,330
GRF	1974	6	bronze	(70 mm)	13,664
GRF	1974	7	silver	(70 mm)	12

NELSON A.
ROCKEFELLER

(VICE PRESIDENT)

1974

When Gerald Ford succeeded Richard Nixon as President in August 1974, that automatically created a new vacancy in the vice presidency. Ford nominated Nelson A. Rockefeller, the former governor of New York, to that post, and Rockefeller, like his predecessor, underwent close scrutiny by committees of the Senate and the House of Representatives before they voted to confirm him as the forty-first Vice President of the United States. He took the oath on December 19, 1974.

Not until mid-January, 1975, did those who had commissioned the Ford presidential and vice-presidential medals take up the question of striking a medal to commemorate Rockefeller. Senator Hatfield had borne the principal burdens in commissioning the Ford medals, and he was reluctant to start anew with Rockefeller. After talking it over with a committee member, Hatfield agreed that a Rockefeller medal should be struck and, on behalf of the committee, which had now assumed an ad hoc status, Hatfield called on Rockefeller at his new office. Rockefeller was too busy to see the Senator. This was January 14.

Two days later, Hatfield wrote him a formal letter, asking permission to strike a medal marking his inauguration as Vice President. Hatfield reminded Rockefeller of a visit he had made to Hatfield's office prior to his confirmation as Vice President, at which time they had discussed striking a special medal for Rockefeller. In his letter, Hatfield explained how the medal would be commissioned and distributed, and he added that the Vice President would designate the charity or cause to receive the royalties.

Rockefeller did not reply to the letter. Weeks went by, and then more weeks. A member of Hatfield's ad hoc committee contacted a member of Rockefeller's staff and informed him that the Vice President owed at least a response to so distinguished a Senator. Not until mid-March did Rockefeller reply, and then he agreed to have the medal struck.

Hatfield immediately called a meeting of the new medals committee on March 14. The two Senators from New York, Jacob Javits and James L. Buckley, had replaced the two Senators from Michigan, and Rockefeller asked that two women prominent in New York art circles be added. Most of the other members had served on the Ford committees.

Rockefeller had a wide reputation as an art patron and collector, and because of that the members of the committee discussed ways to break out of the conventional form the inaugural medals had taken over the years. Senator Javits argued that the Rockefeller medal should be of modern design, possibly in free form. Mrs. Clain-Stefanelli agreed in principle but cautioned against jarring the collecting public with too free a form. The view among committee members was that, with Rockefeller, they had a chance to take artistic liberties certain to be scotched by a subject presumably less familiar with modern art.

They decided to ask for bids from three private mints: the Medallic Art Company, the Franklin Mint, and Medal Arts. Each was told that the committee members wanted to consider dramatic innovations from the traditional form of inaugural medals, and each was asked to submit proposals for a meeting on April 2.

The Franklin Mint had no interest in bidding, but officials of the other two firms made presentations. James Harper of Medal Arts proposed a rectangular medal, as well as an optional circular medal. He suggested three different reverses for the rectangular medal, one quite dramatic. William Louth of the Medallic Art Company offered four models with Rockefeller's portrait by Frank Eliscu (1912—), and the committee members clearly preferred Eliscu's work and Louth's company. They wanted a boldly high relief, and Louth pledged that. They wanted Eliscu's effigy of Rockefeller moved dramatically to one side of the medal and asked that the artist submit two reverses, one of United States flags, the other of an eagle in motion.

The committee members had become disturbed at criticism that too many variants of the inaugural medals had been offered to the public. They voted to confine the Rockefeller medal to the traditional bronze at two-and-three-quarters inches, the antique silver at two-and-a-half inches, and the gold at one-and-a-quarter inches.

Eliscu worked swiftly at his Connecticut studio-home. He wanted a sitting from Rockefeller, but already too much time had elapsed since his inauguration. The sculptor had another difficulty. The Vice President was sixty-six years old. Eliscu felt a sensitivity about portraying him that old. "If you portray every wrinkle," he quipped, "you get a piece of taxidermy." As he explained to a member of the medals committee, he wanted to show the Vice President in his full manhood, his middle years, somewhere indefinitely between forty and sixty-six years of age. What he wanted to achieve, he said, was a "timelessness" of Rockefeller in his maturity. Eliscu had never met him, although he had seen him at close range, and he modelled his portrait with the help of photographs. He placed Rockefeller's effigy on the right side of the obverse, and to enhance its high relief, he modelled the portrait on a convex form. He showed Rockefeller with eyeglasses. "People feel they know him with his glasses on," he said. He gave the Vice President a resolved, determined expression, his eyes piercing and unwavering, the jaw jutting. "Everything I do is slightly exaggerated to heighten the viewer's sensibilities," he said. "A life mask won't look as much like a person as what an artist will do. A living face changes moment to moment."

For the reverse, Eliscu tried several eagles before deciding. He used an eagle with wings poised, screaming defiance and standing on a rocky crag. The image was impressionistic, and "not ornithologically correct," as he stated. To portray the eagle as nature made it would destroy the effect he wanted: strength and defiance. Eliscu saw a symbolism in this design: the United States was much beset in the world and at home, and he meant the eagle to suggest that no one should take America lightly or carelessly.

He had his models completed by mid-April, and the medals committee approved them enthusiastically. The designs were not free form, but Eliscu had achieved a strong, sensitive portrait of the Vice President, in bold relief, and a dramatic reverse to complement it.

On April 22, Senator Hatfield showed the models to Rockefeller for his approval. The committee had voted for high-relief medals, two-and-three-quarters inches in bronze, two-and-a-half inches in silver. To Hatfield's shocked surprise, Rockefeller wanted no such medals. He rejected the high relief immediately, and said that he wanted only a medal in coin relief, about the size of a silver dollar.

"We'll strike you one," Hatfield said.

"I'll need more than that," Rockefeller said. He told Hatfield what he wanted: a dollar-size medal that he could carry in his pocket and give to friends or chance persons he met.

At hazard suddenly was the entire concept of the Rockefeller inaugural medal. Hatfield found himself arguing strenuously for the integrity of Eliscu's work and the committee's decisions and recommendations: there was a tradition on these medals that simply could not be ignored. With Rockefeller's reputation as a knowledgeable art patron, Hatfield never expected this response from him. Hatfield offered to strike as many coin-relief, dollar-size medals as Rockefeller wanted, but the regular-sized inaugural medals in bronze and silver could not be rejected. Only reluctantly did the Vice President give way. He insisted, however, that his portrait be moved traditionally to the center of the medal's obverse, that the lettering of his name be reduced, and that the relief be lowered by placing the portrait on a flat, not rounded surface. "Well," he said to the Senator, "I'm only doing this for you." Hatfield had barely saved the inaugural medal, in traditional size, from Rockefeller's objections.

Eliscu readjusted the portrait to meet the Vice President's demands, and he also made models in coin relief, the lowest relief possible, of the small inaugural medals to be struck to Rockefeller's orders. A medal in coin relief is struck only once, as compared to the multiple strikes required for a high-relief medal. The committee agreed to have these low-relief, one-and-a-half-inch medals made exclusively for Rockefeller. The bronze inaugural medal took five strikes of the powerful presses to bring out the detail.

Senator Hatfield and members of his committee gave Vice President Rockefeller his medal in gold on July 23, 1975, a full seven months and more after his inauguration. Curiously, Rockefeller had forgotten his own criticisms, and he was delighted with the high relief that Eliscu had achieved. Indeed, Rockefeller liked the high-relief medal so much that he lost all interest in the coin-relief medals that he had originally requested. In fact, he decided against ordering any. The Medallic Art Company had made dies from Eliscu's coin-relief models and struck samples for the Vice President in silver and bronze. Later, with the committee's permission, the

Rockefeller Vice-Presidential inaugural medal
Frank Eliscu
Gold, 63 mm
Mrs. Nelson A. Rockefeller

company made a dozen each of these medals in bronze, antique silver, and proof silver, and distributed them to Rockefeller, members of the committee, and others.

As part of its sales program, the company sent an extensive mailing to collectors around the country. Included in the package was a plastic replica of the first version of Eliscu's portrait. A little later, the firm sent to retail dealers the first of the Rockefeller medals struck in bronze as promotion ideas. These were stamped "SAMPLE" on their rims, and, of course, amount to a die variety.

Medals made at Rockefeller's request for his own distribution, but later rejected by him. Private collection

The committee originally voted to limit the silver medals to 5,000, to sell at $75 each, and the gold to 1,500, to sell at $425 each. The bronze medals, priced at $12.50 each, were sold in an unlimited edition. Sales were disappointing: only 935 gold medals and only 2,410 in silver, less than half of the number authorized. The company sold 5,098 in bronze. It struck 15 of these medals in silver with the two-and-three-quarter-inch dies for members of the committee and others.

NAR	1974	1	gold	(63 mm)	1
NAR	1974	2	silver	(63 mm)	2,410
NAR	1974	3	bronze	(70 mm)	5,098
NAR	1974	4	silver	(70 mm)	15
NAR	1974	5	bronze	(38 mm)	12
NAR	1974	6	antique silver	(38 mm)	12
NAR	1974	7	proof silver	(38 mm)	12
NAR	1974	8	bronze "SAMPLE"	(70 mm)	3
NAR	1974	9	gold	(31 mm)	935

JIMMY CARTER
1977

Long before election day, 1976, those responsible began planning for the inauguration of the successful candidate. In September, by request, President Ford and Jimmy Carter, his Democratic opponent, each named the persons to take charge if he won. Carter chose two: Bardyl R. Tirana, a Washington lawyer, and Vicki Rogers of South Carolina, both Carter campaign volunteers. When Carter won, they became the first co-chairpersons of an inauguration and Miss Rogers the first woman so designated. The Medallic Art Company and its rival, the Franklin Mint, also took early action. Medallic commissioned six sculptors to model portraits of the two candidates. Franklin asked Julian Hoke Harris (1906—), a Georgian, to sculpt a relief of Carter. These advance preparations made possible the earliest decision ever on the new President's medal.

The Ford and Carter representatives met separately with executives of the two mints on October 28, the Thursday before election day. Tirana had studied previous inaugurations, Nixon's in 1973 closely, and he wanted to operate differently. The Carter inauguration would not use the traditional Guarantee Fund. Tirana would need money. Carter had indicated to him that he wanted a traditional inauguration, but simple, democratic, and unpretentious. Tirana also was familiar with inaugural medals: his law partner, Bruce Sundlun, had chaired the 1961 and 1965 medals committees.

Tirana told both firms that if Carter were elected, he would act promptly. "I won't have to consult with anyone else," he said. "Governor Carter does in fact delegate authority." He asked both to submit their proposals as soon as possible. He had $93,000 in carry-over from the 1973 inauguration, and he reminded them that Franklin had put up $1,000,000 in advance that year. Tirana intended to use the medals to finance his initial operations instead of the Guarantee Fund: it was a new role for the President's medal.

Design did not concern Tirana; he counted on the mint to produce a worthy medal. "I did not want to subject my taste, my artistic preferences, on the public." He saw no reason to name a medals committee. "Why have one?" he asked. He did want the mint chosen to handle all phases of the medals program, from design and production to promotion and distribution, to relieve his committee of those chores. "I was not worried about artistic merit," he said. The President-elect and his advisers would approve the model.

The Medallic team, headed by Donald Schwartz, believed they could not outbid Franklin. Discouraged, Schwartz went on vacation, leaving negotiations to an aide. Franklin's negotiators, led by Frank Fitzpatrick, were more cautious than Schwartz suspected. They could see in the final, official accounting of their 1973 contract that they had paid royalties far higher than originally believed: a surprising 34 percent. This was because they had given so many items free to the committee: 250 silver plates and 4,750 silver and bronze medals. This reduced actual gross revenues from the assumed $3,533,000 to $3,227,587. At 20 percent royalty, they should have paid $645,517, not the $1,000,000 advanced. These figures now cooled Franklin's negotiators. Tirana had flown to Atlanta on election day, and they joined him there the next day, after Carter won. They offered an advance of $750,000, against 20 percent royalties, provided he obtained for them the United States Mint's list of bicentennial medal-buyers. "Suppose I can't get the list?" Tirana asked. "We'll give you $500,000," Fitzpatrick said. That was how they drew the contract. It took effect November 5, just three days after Carter's election, and it authorized Franklin to strike proof and antique silver and bronze medals in the usual sizes, and small gold medals. In addition, Franklin produced eight-inch silver plates, small charms in gold and silver, a crystal paperweight, and first-day "philatelic-numismatic" covers with small silver medals, all with the portrait. Fitzpatrick ordered four gold medals, two-and-three-quarters inches in diameter, struck for President Carter, Vice President Walter Mondale, and the inaugural co-chairpersons.

Harris worked from photographs to create a sixteen-inch model in plaster, which Franklin reduced for the dies. Harris had earlier modelled another portrait of Carter, in three-quarters profile: Franklin's 1976 Democratic campaign medal. Harris knew Carter, and he drew him with "a concentrated brow and pleasant mouth." He decided against showing Carter's famed toothy smile: "I wanted him thinking about something." At first Harris was asked to use Carter's given names, James Earl. "They changed it back to 'Jimmy,'" he said. "Nobody knows him by anything else." The reverse, the presidential seal, was modelled at the Franklin Mint.

JC	1977	1	gold	(70 mm)	4
JC	1977	2	proof silver	(63 mm)	
JC	1977	3	antique silver	(63 mm)	
JC	1977	4	proof bronze	(70 mm)	
JC	1977	5	antique bronze	(70 mm)	
JC	1977	6	gold	(32 mm)	

INDEX

The name of an artist appears in parentheses after the President's name.